CLEMATIS

For Everyone

Raymond J. Evison

floramedia

First published 2000 by
Burall Floraprint Limited, Wisbech, UK

A fully revised sequel to "Making the Most of Clematis",
originally published in the UK by Floraprint Limited, Nottingham
Copyright © Burall Floraprint Limited, 2000

A CIP catalogue record for this book is available from the British Library

ISBN 0 903001 70 5

Floramedia books are published by
Burall Floraprint Limited, Wisbech, UK
e-mail: floramedia@burall.com
website: www.floramedia.co.uk

Picture Credits
All photographs by the author or Burall Floraprint with the following exceptions:
Harry Smith Collection, Front Cover, pages 9, 30, 44, 55
Neil Campbell-Sharp, pages 41, 57, 83
Garden Picture Library, page 37
John Elsley, pages 62, 64, 65
Sarah Sage, page 3

Page 1 and chapter pages: Clematis **Josephine**™ 'Evijohill'®
Front Cover: Clematis *macropetala* var. *macropetala*
Front Cover inset: Raymond Evison with Clematis **Liberation**™ 'Evifive'®

Line drawings by Christine Sampson

Printed in Singapore

Foreword

Raymond Evison has been involved with the genus Clematis for nearly 40 years. During this time he has built up a collection of over 500 species and cultivars. In recent years, he has been fortunate enough to travel widely; his lecturing engagements have taken him as far afield as China, Japan, Poland, Latvia, Estonia, the United States and Canada, where he has had the opportunity of searching for clematis species and cultivars in nurseries, gardens and in the wild – his greatest love.

His nursery in Guernsey, is one of the largest clematis production nurseries in the world, producing clematis for the wholesale markets throughout the world. From there he has introduced many species and cultivars to provide gardeners worldwide with an ever-increasing choice of clematis.

In 1984 Raymond Evison founded the International Clematis Society and in 1989 became the Society's first President.

He has been much involved with the work of the National Council for the Conservation of Plants and Gardens. He was a member of Council of the Royal Horticultural Society from 1985 to 1996, is a Fellow of the Institute of Horticulture and was awarded the Victoria Medal of Honour by the RHS in 1995 for his outstanding service to British Horticulture. Again for his services to horticulture, Raymond received the OBE in The Queen's New Year's Honours List, January 2000.

His knowledge of clematis is based on years of practical experience and is blended with a love of plants which must be obvious to all those who have attended his lectures.

Acknowledgments

The author would like to record his deep gratitude to Diana Rowland in the preparation of this book, 'Clematis for Everyone'. He would also like to express his thanks to Mary Shirville of the National Association of Flower Arrangement Societies for her helpful comments on the chapter 'Clematis as a Cut Flower'. He would also like to thank both John Elsley, Greenwood South Carolina and Tom Hawkins, Florasource, California for their help and advice in the preparation of the chapter 'Growing Clematis in North America' and in particular to John Elsley for his advice in making the hardiness zones recommendations. Finally he would like to thank his editor, Elspeth Houghton, for her professionalism and endurance in putting the final touches to the book.

Clematis 'Nelly Moser', an old favourite

Clematis texensis 'Princess Diana' (syn. 'The Princess of Wales')

Clematis Alabast™ *'Poulala'®, one of the newer cream cultivars*

Contents

An Introduction to Clematis

The extent of the range of clematis available today – differing size and colour of flowers, flowering period, the type of growth, variations in foliage, etc. – gives the gardener a bewildering choice when selecting which species or cultivar to plant where and with what. But it does allow the imaginative gardener and plantsman an unlimited freedom of choice of planting site, colour combination and plant association. Creating a colour scheme with foliage and flower as if an artist: not with a brush but with living plants; not on a canvas but in a garden! What could be more exciting or rewarding?

The genus clematis (pronounced klem-<u>a</u>-tis – '<u>a</u>' as in 'ado') is a most rewarding and fascinating group of plants which varies enormously throughout the world in the shape and formation of flowers, leaves and leaflets.

Most of the species native to the northern hemisphere are deciduous, the exceptions being the evergreen Mediterranean C. *cirrhosa* and its forms, together with the Chinese evergreens such as *armandii*, *uncinata* and *meyeniana*. The southern hemisphere greatly extends the range of both deciduous and evergreen species. However, it is the charming New Zealand species, such as C. *australis*, *forsteri* and *paniculata* that are the most

useful and attractive. Sadly, these are not entirely winter hardy in cold northern European or North American gardens, but they are most successful if grown in conservatories or garden rooms, adding colour and, in some cases, scent.

The flowers of the species vary dramatically in form and shape, from the nodding, pitcher-shaped flowers of the American clematis, through the small bell and star-shaped flowers of the European clematis, to the large flat erectly-held flowers of the species *patens* which hails from China and has naturalised in Japan. In addition to these there is the important and great

wealth of species in all forms that are native to the Himalayan mountain range such as C. *montana* and *tangutica*, and the herbaceous or sub-shrub forms of clematis from China such as *heracleifolia* var. *davidiana* with its hyacinth-like flowers.

This great variation of the species extends to the cultivar and large-flowered clematis that have been produced during the last one hundred and sixty years, many of which are still amongst the most popular cultivars of modern gardens. The first cultivar, C. 'Eriostemon', was raised in Holland in 1830 and was thought to be the result of a cross between C. *integrifolia* and

China, Japan and the Himalayas are home to a wealth of clematis species.

Clematis montana 'Broughton Star' is unusual but still most attractive.

Clematis montana f. grandiflora.

These three clematis are from Group One. Clematis montana 'Pink Perfection' on the left is easily recognisable and widely available.

C. viticella, both European species, the former being a herbaceous clematis. The resultant cultivar was a tall-growing non-clinging plant, still grown in present-day gardens.

For the more technically minded there are over three hundred clematis species distributed throughout the world. This book will be concerned mainly with the species and their cultivars which are native to the northern hemisphere, along with their cultivation and uses in a modern garden whether it be formal, informal,

patio or the natural woodland garden. The robust species clematis can be allowed to run riot in a natural woodland garden, enjoying life to the full with the freedom to ramble and climb without restriction.

Regrettably, many of the three hundred species have no, or at least little garden value, and are of interest only to the clematis collector, botanist or hybridist. However, their presence has given rise to the very splendid cultivars of today.

Three main groups

The clematis of important garden value that are offered for sale and grown in their millions today may be divided into three main groups. The splitting and grouping is used purely for the convenience of cultivation, the ease of identifying the flowering habits, and most of all the pruning requirements.

Group One consists of the charming species and their cultivars which produce their main batch of flowers in early spring. The flowers are produced on short flower stalks directly from the leaf axil bud, generally on the previous season's ripened stems. This group has a range of species, including the evergreen forms which flower first of all, the charming *alpina* and *macropetala* types flower next and our old reliable friend *montana* follows closely behind, although its rampaging nature is so unlike the more compact habit of the evergreen forms and the alpines.

Group Two cultivars also produce their flowers from stems which grew the previous year and became ripened before the autumn frosts. The ripened leaf axil buds produce strong new stems which may vary in length, depending upon the cultivar, from 10–30cm or even 60cm each, with a single large flower at the growing tip.

This group consists of the early large-flowered cultivars such as 'Nelly Moser' and 'The President', the strange doubles and semi-doubles such as 'Vyvyan Pennell', and the very large-flowered cultivars such as 'Marie Boisselot' which start flowering before mid summer.

Group Three clematis flower on new growth from mid summer onwards – all the previous season's stems become almost useless and die away naturally each autumn. This group of clematis are most useful garden plants and vary from the large open flowers of the Jackmanii types to the starry-shaped flowers of some of the European species to the dainty nodding flowers of the yellow C. *aethusifolia* from China. The interesting clematis of herbaceous habit also fit into this group, varying in flower and foliage from the delightful urn-shaped flowers of some of the North American species to the nodding European species of *integrifolia* and the hyacinth-like flowers of the *heraclei-folia* types which are native to China and Japan.

These are two clematis from Group Two. Clematis 'Vyvyan Pennell' top, Clematis 'Elsa Späth' below. Although their colouring is similar, the tepal shapes are quite different, as can be seen here.

*These are two clematis from Group Three. Clematis 'Madame Baron Veillard' on the left is an old and easily recognised cultivar, while Clematis **Petit Faucon**™ 'Evisix'® is a stunning new cultivar.*

Flower colours and form

The selection of flower form and flowering habit is indeed extensive and the variation in flower colour is quite fascinating. The delicate shades to choose from are mostly pastel colours, not overpowering or too loud, allowing freedom of colour association with other plants and flowers. Purple, blue and mauve are the predominant colours, although regrettably the blue is not a clear blue as with a delphinium which is a close relative of the clematis, both being members of the Ranunculaceae family.

The reds also are not a pure colour since the nearest true red contains shades of blue or purple, but they blend perfectly with most garden planting schemes. The pinks are refreshing and are of various pastel shades, frequently having two tones, giving a bar or star-like appearance as with the ever popular 'Nelly Moser', whose blossoms are often described as resembling small cartwheels. Even the deepest shades of pink fade gently in bright sunlight and are therefore not ideal for a sunny, south-facing position. This can, however, be used to advantage because the early-flowering pinks are ideal for brightening up a dull north-facing position where the sun's rays do not reach the freshly opened flowers, thus avoiding premature fading.

A large-flowered, deep buttercup yellow clematis is yet to be produced; and for the time being, the yellows are represented by the deep yellow, nodding flowers of C. *tangutica* var. *tangutica*. For the gardener with a little imagination, the creamy-yellow flowers of 'Guernsey Cream' and 'Wada's Primrose' are, of course, deep yellow! Both of these cultivars are most delightful and, if grown in a north, west or east-facing position will retain their creamy yellow colours better than if planted in full sunlight.

The white-flowered clematis are very elegant and some of my favourite clematis are amongst the whites. Many of the large-flowered cultivars have such a pure colouring, and the starry-flowered species look superb if allowed to grow through dark foliaged evergreens, such as hollies and pines. The colourful part of a clematis flower is not called a petal, as with most garden flowers, but a tepal. The petals are absent, except in the case of some of the *alpina* and *macropetala* clematis which have petaloid stamens. Many garden flowers such as the rose have green tepals and colourful petals, the tepals protecting and guarding the delicate petals as they form in the flower bud before the flower opens.

Greening of flowers

During a season when plants are late in producing their flowers due to bad weather conditions, some clematis flowers often open green, the correct colour appearing later as the flowers age and the tepals are subjected to the sun's rays. Often, if this occurs, the flowers do not completely attain the true colour, the centre of the tepal remaining slightly green. This is almost certain to occur with white, or very pale pink or pale blue cultivars.

The very early flowering cultivars of the early large-flowered section such as 'Edith' or 'Dawn' (Group Two) should be planted where they will receive some direct sunlight. They should not be planted in a cold north-facing position. The varieties susceptible to the unwanted greening of flowers are noted in the Glossary on pages 78 to 122 and are not recommended for a north-facing position. These green flowers are delightful if one is a keen flower arranger, or has a taste for the unusual. A plant of 'Moonlight' that I once grew through a *Garrya elliptica*, which was on a cold north-east facing position, always produced its first flowers during cold springs in a delicate shade of green. These never failed to arouse interest with visitors to my garden.

Scent

We are fortunate in having a small selection of clematis which give a pleasant scent; regrettably, even with the wildest imagination and on the warmest spring evening, this perfume cannot be compared with that of a

During some seasons, because of irratic weather conditions, the tepals do not attain their true colour, as this flower of Clematis 'Barbara Dibley' shows.

rose. The species *flammula*, which is a native of the northern Mediterranean shoreline, is perhaps the hardiest of the strong-scented clematis species that can be grown and flowered in northern British and European gardens. The hardiest of all the strong-scented species known to me must be the "Sweet Autumn Scented Clematis" grown widely in American gardens. *C. terniflora* (my American friends still incorrectly call it *C. paniculata*) does not flower well for us in northern British and European gardens. Our summers are neither hot enough nor long enough for it to perform well.

The strongest scented clematis species that I have grown is one that I have known as a form of *C. forsteri*, a New Zealand species. Many of the species from New Zealand have hybridized in the wild and there is some confusion over their names.

Recently, cultivars have also been produced in England. However, my *C. forsteri*, which needs to be grown in a conservatory or cold glasshouse, has the most delightful scent (that of lemon verbena perhaps). It is very free flowering and is a must for the conservatory.

Another strong-growing species with a good scent and white flowers that I have grown for a few years is *C. brachiata* from South Africa which flowers towards the autumn. It needs a very sheltered spot, as does the Tasmanian species *C. gentianoides* which flowers well with protection in the early spring. The European species, *C. integrifolia* var. *integrifolia*, has forms that are scented. *C. integrifolia* 'Alba', which I am growing for the first time, has a delightful, strong scent.

Another European species *recta* var. *recta*, a clematis of herbaceous

Clematis × triternata 'Rubromarginata' has gorgeous hawthorn-like scent.

habit, has a very sickly sweet scent which is so heavy it is nearly unpleasant. A delightful, pale pink *montana* cultivar called 'Elizabeth' has a most heavenly scent when in full flower at the end of April. On a warm evening one is sometimes tempted to linger in one's garden with the scent of 'Elizabeth' until the moon rises! However a fairly new introduction *montana* 'Mayleen' with pink rounded flowers is the strongest scented of all the *montanas* that I grow.

A few of the large-flowered clematis have a woody scent – that perhaps of violets – but one's imagination is most definitely needed with all of these, with the exception of 'Fair Rosamund'. Unfortunately her flowers are a washy pink or off-white, not the best of clematis from the point

of view of flowering or long performance, but still worthy of garden space. The foliage of *C. heracleifolia* var. *davidiana* when it becomes dry during the early part of winter is very heavily scented.

Attachment of clematis to host plant

The genus clematis offers such a wide variety of flowering habit, size, shape and colour of bloom, even a selection of scented forms, that one wonders what other attributes can remain. As far as I am aware there is only one other, and that is the manner by which clematis attach themselves to their host. The clematis, unlike other natural climbers, does not attach itself by sucker pads as does a virginia creeper, or with aerial roots as in the case of

the ivy, and it does not strangle its host. It twists its leaf stalk (petiole) gently around the nearest support, securing itself against anything except the strongest of gales.

The gentle attachment of most species and cultivars is embarrassed only by the over-vigorous nature of the *montana* family, which if allowed to ramble up a wall on to a roof is quite likely to gently, but forcibly, remove any tiles as it searches for suitable supports and light. The weight of growth when an established *montana* is in full foliage has also been responsible for bringing down telephone wires – so be warned, keep your *montana* family under control!

An Introduction to Clematis

Site, Soil and Aspects of Planting

The planting position of a clematis in relationship to its host or support and the thorough preparation of the planting site are vitally important. Obviously, if the correct choice of clematis species or cultivar has been made, and it is then planted without thought or correct soil preparation, all will be lost; or, at best, life could be made extremely difficult for the unfortunate clematis. Plain common sense and a little gardening knowledge are all that is necessary. I do not intend to give strict instructions, but simply describe some of the pitfalls, and advise on the most successful methods I have found regarding soil requirements.

A clematis will undoubtedly be expected to grace its host or support for many years to come, barring accidents of course. So, if the reader spends even as much as one hour on the planting site, religiously carrying out the advice that I am about to give, if not insist upon, then that time is little in comparison with the many pleasurable years ahead.

I must be honest regarding one clematis that I planted (or rather did not plant) which now adorns a wall-trained shrub, *Garrya elliptica*, on a bone-dry strip of soil at the base of a cold east-facing wall. Through the *Garrya* grows *Clematis* 'Moonlight' most successfully. No thought or soil preparation took place: the clematis

was simply placed under the shrub and inadvertently forgotten. When I finally remembered, the clematis had firmly rooted itself into the soil through the thin paper pot it had been grown in. I apologised and gave the plant nine litres (two gallons) of water and it has never looked back and has flowered well every year since.

Planting Position

When considering the planting position, it is wise to think and remember where the most successful clematis species grow in their wild habitat. The species produces many thousands of seeds annually, many germinate and start into life in various places even in what may appear to be bone-dry cracks in a rock face. However, one dry summer and disaster strikes! The most successful seedlings establish themselves underneath the overhanging branches of a shrub or tree where their requirements will be satisfied. The host's branches will shade the clematis roots just below the soil surface, at the same time allowing sufficient rainfall to penetrate to the root system, and the clematis vines can attach themselves to the host plant. This simple lesson from nature, of where the clematis survives best in the wild, should be used as a guideline when planting in our modern gardens. In fact, very often when I have been

looking for clematis species in the wild, especially in China and Japan, I have found them growing out from underneath rocks, stones and scree. Sometimes when I have traced the clematis plant's main stem to find its root system, it has been buried beneath as much as 60cm or more of stones and scree giving the plants plenty of shade and, of course, moisture. I do not suggest that we should cover up our clematis plant's root system to that degree, but it is a point worth remembering.

No clematis in the wild would flourish or perhaps even survive if planted within a few centimetres of the base of a wall in a bone-dry strip of soil (unless the gardener has "green fingers"). Likewise, it would be difficult for a clematis to establish itself at the base of a tree with a large trunk which would be surrounded with very dry soil. It is possible to establish a strong-growing clematis species in such a site, but it does take time, patience and lots of water. It would also be foolish to attempt to grow a clematis if its root system had to compete for every drop of moisture and natural food from the soil with the hungry feeder roots of a small tree or shrub. *Laburnum*, hawthorn and lilac can be perfect hosts but their hungry root systems have to be overcome by the correct planting position, soil

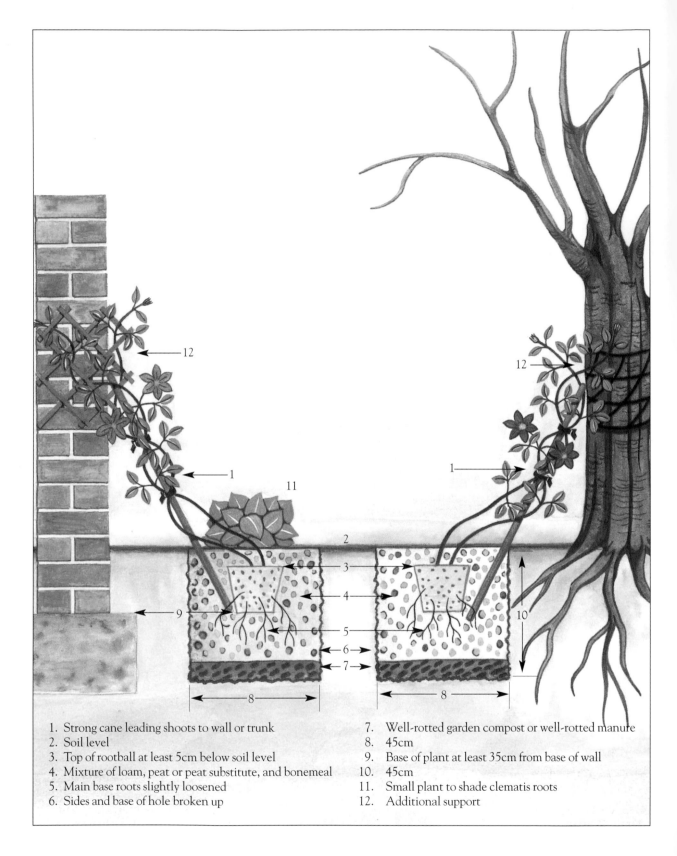

1. Strong cane leading shoots to wall or trunk
2. Soil level
3. Top of rootball at least 5cm below soil level
4. Mixture of loam, peat or peat substitute, and bonemeal
5. Main base roots slightly loosened
6. Sides and base of hole broken up
7. Well-rotted garden compost or well-rotted manure
8. 45cm
9. Base of plant at least 35cm from base of wall
10. 45cm
11. Small plant to shade clematis roots
12. Additional support

Planting a clematis against a wall and a tree

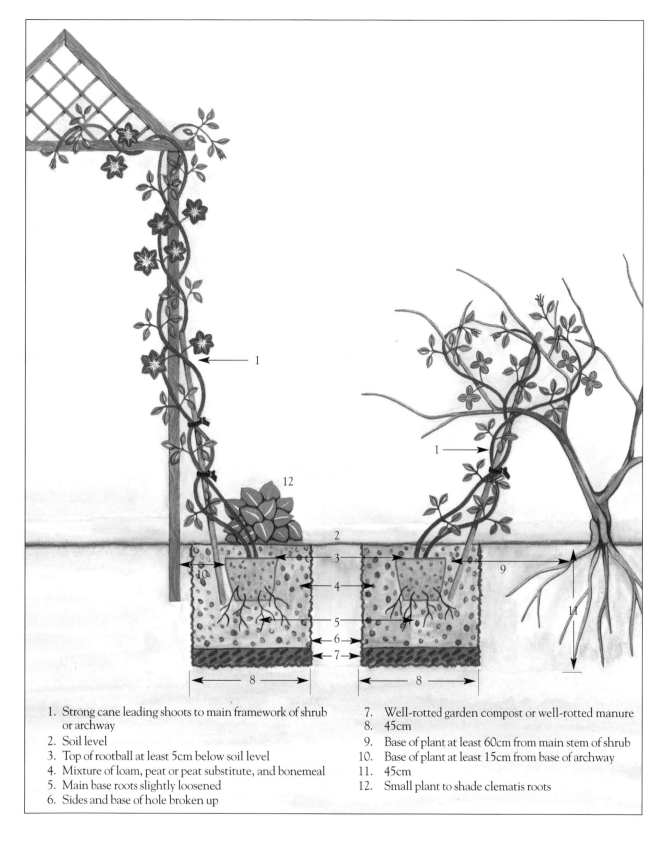

1. Strong cane leading shoots to main framework of shrub or archway
2. Soil level
3. Top of rootball at least 5cm below soil level
4. Mixture of loam, peat or peat substitute, and bonemeal
5. Main base roots slightly loosened
6. Sides and base of hole broken up
7. Well-rotted garden compost or well-rotted manure
8. 45cm
9. Base of plant at least 60cm from main stem of shrub
10. Base of plant at least 15cm from base of archway
11. 45cm
12. Small plant to shade clematis roots

Planting a clematis against an archway and a shrub.

Clematis 'Hagley Hybrid' is a later flowering, large flowered hybrid.

preparation and sufficient watering after planting.

Soil Preparation

It is advisable on all but the most perfect soils to carry out some soil preparation before planting. The exact site has been chosen, now the hard work begins. A hole, to a depth of 45cm with a diameter also no less than 45cm, should be dug, removing the good topsoil and placing it in a different place from the subsoil from the base of the hole. The subsoil must be disposed of but the good topsoil can be used again when refilling the hole.

If the soil is a very heavy clay, and soil preparation takes place during wet weather conditions, the sides of the hole will compact and appear like an impenetrable concrete wall to the young feeder clematis roots. So, before replacing the fresh soil, the side and bottom of the hole must be broken up as it is vital that no firm flat surfaces are left surrounding the hole. If the base of the hole is also not broken up this may retain too much rainwater and the clematis roots will possibly spend part of each winter with very cold frozen roots, which may decay causing a great deal of damage.

Back to the important hole! Before it is refilled, two forkfuls of well rotted farmyard manure, or well decayed garden compost, if available, should be placed at the bottom of the hole and lightly forked in; this rich compost or manure must be kept away from the young clematis roots and placed only at the bottom of the hole. Mix two bucketfuls of peat or peat substitute and two handfuls of sterilized bonemeal with the retained topsoil, place into the hole and lightly firm using one's feet. If, when removing the soil from the planting site, the topsoil is found to be extremely poor then this can be replaced by using old John Innes potting soil, or a mixture of equal proportions of loam, peat, sand and grit. When planting on very heavy clay soil, or very porous sandy soil, additional peat or peat substitute may be used giving the newly planted clematis every chance of quick and safe establishment in its new site. When refilling the hole, replace with a little extra soil to allow for sinkage.

When to plant

The best months of the year for planting clematis previously established in a container are the spring or the autumn months when gardening in Central Europe but in warmer climates this will be somewhat earlier and in cold areas such as North America or Scandinavia where spring arrives later, planting will need to be delayed.

One must not rule out the remaining months. Clematis planted during mid-summer or mid-winter if the soil conditions are favourable, will establish satisfactorily, but require much more attention. Nearly all clematis plants supplied by nurserymen are grown in containers and therefore can be planted throughout the year without causing distress to the plant, as long as sufficient water is applied to the freshly planted clematis during very dry weather conditions.

If a clematis is planted during the early spring the plant will establish itself easily during what is the natural period of growth for a clematis but it is important that the plant receives sufficient water until it becomes established. It may take five or six weeks before the feeder roots have become rooted into the compost provided in the planting site. Until this time moisture can only be gained from the root ball that existed before planting and water supplied by the gardener. As with other plants, do not just water the area where the stem emerges from the soil, water the surrounding area to a diameter of at least 30cm as this will then encourage the roots to grow into the surrounding soil as they look for and find the moisture provided.

Planted with its roots in the shade Clematis texensis 'Pagoda' will flower from July to September.

When planting clematis during the summer months, it is vital for the plant's survival that it receives at least 4.5 litres (one gallon) of water per day during dry weather. The soil must be moist and stick to the fingers when touched. Check the soil 8cm from the surface. If only dusty soil remains on your fingers the clematis requires water, and this could be for a period of eight weeks until the root system becomes established into its new surroundings. It would be my advice that the planting of clematis in hot climates should not be attempted during the summer months.

If planting is carried out during the early autumn, the safer and easier life becomes for the establishment of your clematis. Unless the summer has been especially dry, the soil should still hopefully be warm from the summer months and this will encourage quick root establishment. Clematis plants normally stop producing foliage from early autumn onwards until the next season but the root systems continue growing until the winter becomes cold and the soil temperatures drop low.

During mild winters when conditions allow the gardener to cultivate the soil, clematis may also be planted. The plant will merely exist and not attempt to establish itself until the soil temperature rises and daylight hours increase. It is not advisable to plant evergreens, or the less vigorous species and cultivars during the winter months. Even species such as *alpina*, *montana* and *tangutica* quite often will fail if they have to exist for several months immediately after planting in

Once the root system has been thoroughly soaked, place the rootball into a hole so that it is buried at least 5cm below soil level.

healthy foliage and a thick stem at the base of the plant, then this type of plant will grow satisfactorily. The smaller plant will just take a little longer to gain maturity since one buys time when planting a larger plant.

For successful establishment it does not matter whether or not the plant is in flower when bought. If the clematis is purchased during the late summer months, or early autumn, the leaves may be starting to die off, because most clematis are deciduous. If a clematis is bought during the winter, old leaves may still be left on the plant and to all appearances the plant may look dead. To check this the leaf axil buds should be visible by this time and will give a guideline to the plant's health and possible performance during the following summer. The choice of plant should be one that has several strong swelling leaf axil buds at the base of the stem (not at the top). With the late-flowering species and cultivars, especially the Jackmanii group, the new growth will appear right at the base of the previous season's growth, or even from below the soil level in the container.

Planting a young clematis

Before removing the plant from its container, submerge it in a bucket of water for 15 to 20 minutes; this will soak the root system thoroughly and will help the plant until the roots start to take up moisture from the freshly prepared site.

With a trowel dig a hole in the soil large enough to take the root ball (see p16 Soil Preparation), allowing sufficient depth so that the root ball will be buried at least 5cm below soil level. This deeper planting will help in the event of damage during future cultivation or by animals. If damage at soil level should occur in the future the plant will produce new growth from below the soil level from dormant leaf axil buds; thus, in the event that the clematis stem should

very cold wet soils, particularly if the soil is naturally a heavy clay. This can happen even when thorough soil preparation has previously been carried out. However, planting under trees where the soil is drier during these winter months can be an advantage. The soil condition under trees during this period is generally not too wet and can be warmer than an open garden situation, so that the clematis can start into growth as soon as the temperature rises. Hopefully the plant can then be partly on its way towards establishment before the dry spring and summer months when lots of water will be required to make the

plant's life bearable until its roots are firmly growing into the new site. Under some overhanging evergreen trees this establishment could take eighteen months; but be patient, because it is worth the extra effort, and the reward will be yours when the clematis is in full flower.

Choice of plant

When purchasing a clematis from a nurseryman, or garden centre, it is not important that the plant should be the tallest, or the most costly. If the plant is in a pot no smaller than 10cm in diameter, growing on a cane 30–40cm high, is strong in appearance with

When the plant is at the correct depth secure a cane to the host plant to provide good support.

vitalba are all quite distinctive from the large-flowered cultivars. They all have very fine, thread-like root systems when young plants, as compared with the thick bootlace-type of roots of the large-flowered cultivars. If in doubt, don't disturb the root system. The plant can be placed gently into the hole and firmed well by pressing the soil carefully, but firmly, around the root ball.

Initial training

The cane or support to which the clematis stem has been attached in the container must not be removed. Another cane should be placed near the root ball, secured to the existing one and then itself secured to the host plant or support. The main stem of the clematis must have a firm support, otherwise damage may occur through wind.

As the newly planted clematis produces new growth this should be carefully trained and tied into position on the supporting cane until the stems reach the support or the main framework of the host plant or tree. As a firm rule, all newly planted clematis should be pruned down to at least 30cm the first spring after planting. The exact time will depend upon location but it should be before bud break. This almost severe action will be rewarded by a more bushy, compact clematis. It is important that a strong framework of lower stems is established and the young clematis must not be allowed to grow away producing only one or two stems. Admittedly, it is more difficult to achieve a bushy plant of the late-flowering, large-flowered cultivars due to their natural habit of growing from only just above ground level each year. However, hard pruning and pinching out of the young stems of the early-flowering clematis is rewarded in a bushy, compact plant, well furnished with flowers. Give up a few flowers the first year and hope to get double or treble the following years. Be an opti-

become severed, even on a mature plant, the plant will not be lost. This deeper planting will also help and is strongly recommended for another reason: if the clematis plant, at some stage, might suffer from 'clematis wilt', then the more deeply planted clematis will almost certainly grow again from below soil level. More can be found out about the clematis wilt problem on page 76 under Pests and Diseases.

The plant should be removed from its container after the root system has been soaked but do not submerge for longer than 15 to 20 minutes: plants, like humans, can have too much water! The bootlace-like roots of the large-flowered cultivars which are at the base of the container and probably growing in ringlets may be slightly loosened but do not disturb the main root ball as this will be fatal. However, if only a few roots are freed this will help the plant establish much more easily. On no account should the root systems of the fibrous-rooted species, their varieties and cultivars be disturbed and great care must be taken with the root system when planting this type of clematis. The root systems of species such as *tangutica*, *orientalis*, the *alpina* types, *macropetala*, *potanini* var. *fargesii*, *flammula*, *serratifolia* and

mist, as I am with my clematis, and look forward to the future.

Moving an established plant

The replanting of an established garden clematis is always a challenge but with care and a bit of luck it may be achieved. The only time when success can reasonably be expected is during the months of very early spring before bud break when the plant is in its dormant period, or at least just coming out of dormancy.

If the correct pruning procedure has been carried out during the plant's lifetime, a large proportion of the top growth must be removed, ideally down to about 40–60cm. The stems must be cut just above a pair of strong leaf axil buds: do not cut into an old stem that shows no sign of life. Tie the remaining stems to a strong bamboo cane which should be placed firmly near the root crown but beware of new shoots which may be just under the surface of the soil as you will need every leaf axil bud and possible new growth points in the coming months.

Dig a circle around the root crown to spade depth and a diameter of 60cm with the root crown in the centre. Carefully lift the root ball out of the hole, with help from another person: do not be tempted to pull the root ball by the top growth, that would be fatal. Place the root ball onto a sack or polythene sheet, taking care to leave as much soil around the clematis root system as possible. The clematis may then be replanted into its new site, which should be prepared in the same manner as for the young clematis, but of course a larger hole needs to be prepared. The plant should be planted 5cm deeper than in its previous position. The first spring and summer after planting, the soil surrounding the plant must be kept moist at all times – plenty of water. The remaining top growth should be carefully tied into the support at its new site.

The large-flowered cultivars are

This container grown clematis has a healthy root system with bootlace-like roots – when planting gently tease out root tips but do not disturb the main rootball.

the safest plants to re-establish, the fibrous-rooted species the most difficult as their very fine roots drop away as they are being moved and with very little root being retained re-establishment is generally not possible.

Annual feeding and mulching of established plants

For an established clematis which did not receive the ideal soil preparation, additional feed or enrichment of the soil is needed to prevent a slow decline of the plant. The ideal time for feeding clematis is during the very early spring months when the plant needs every bit of food and moisture it can obtain to produce strong healthy foliage and flowers.

Feeding can take various forms. If available in late winter or very early spring, well rotted farmyard manure or well rotted garden compost makes an ideal feeding mulch because not only does the mulch feed the clematis but, if spread thickly enough on the soil above the root system, it will give additional shade to the roots and also enrich the topsoil in the process as the manure decays. The mulch should be placed on the soil near to the main stem of the plant to a depth of 8cm and to a diameter of 50cm. Care must be taken not to place any of the rotted farmyard manure on the main stem or foliage of the plant as this will cause damage. A space of at least 12cm around the stem must be left.

If rotted farmyard manure is not available, a mulch of peat or peat substitute placed in a similar manner will suffice. This should be mixed with sterilised bonemeal at the rate of two handfuls of bonemeal per nine litre (two gallon) bucket of peat. After the mulch has been placed on the soil surface it may be lightly forked in using a small hand fork. Care must be taken not to damage the feeder roots which will be very near to the soil surface. In the event of no rain within two weeks, the mulch should be moistened with at least nine litres (two gallons) of water which will stop the peat from blowing away and will also assist the bonemeal to enter the topsoil and reach the clematis feeder roots.

If mulching is not a practicality, the use of liquid feed is another alternative. There are numerous liquid feeds available and any of the well-known brand-named products can be relied upon. It is important, however, that the liquid feed chosen is a well balanced general feed. The liquid feed can be applied during watering during the spring and early summer months, as per the instructions on the container. If the soil where the clematis is growing is dust dry, the plant must receive at least nine litres (two gallons) of clear water before the liquid feed is applied. It is, however, important that feeding should be stopped just before flowering commences: that is, when flower buds on the most forward flowering stems are the size of a pea. If feeding were to continue during the build-up to full flowering and during flowering, then sadly the flowers would mature much faster, thus reducing the flowering period of the plant.

Clematis 'Carnaby' has its first flush of flowers in early summer and then another at the end of the summer.

Clematis 'Will Goodwin' growing in a container inside a conservatory.

Pruning Techniques

The pruning of clematis is probably the most talked about and written about aspect of clematis cultivation. What is a very basic and simple subject has regrettably been discussed and reviewed in such detail that the pruning of clematis has become unnecessarily complicated, causing confusion to both the experienced gardener and the newcomer to clematis growing.

Nurserymen in preparing their plant lists and catalogues (and I too have been guilty of this) have gone into great detail regarding pruning. Species and cultivars have been listed under different types of clematis, generally according to the large-flowered species from China and Japan (and their cultivated forms) such as *patens*, *florida* or *lanuginosa*. It is these and other species which have given rise to the hundreds of cultivars being produced before the early 1900s. The problems and details increased and became more entangled as new cultivars were produced and offered for sale. Therefore, with every good intention to help and assist their customers and readers, the nursery trade and writers of gardening periodicals have given rise to much unnecessary confusion regarding pruning.

As a gardener gains experience with growing clematis they will try to vary their pruning technique to suit an individual plant's own growth pattern which can change from year to year. Whatever they do, their aim will be to achieve the largest number of good quality flowers and healthy foliage.

After making the initial statement that pruning is a simple exercise, I have carried on to explain that pruning can then be varied from the basic technique as experience is gained; and it is at this point that confusion has occurred, with conflicting opinions being offered to the gardener. My intention, therefore, is to give the reader basic pruning requirements from the first spring after planting for each of the three different groups of clematis which were described on page 8. If you subsequently want to find out which type of basic pruning your own clematis should receive, look up the name of the plant in the Glossary on pages 78 to 122 and there you will find the pruning group specified.

If you are a beginner to clematis growing, the techniques illustrated on page 26 are entirely adequate and I suggest you delay reading my comments on more advanced pruning and training until you feel quite confident with the basic methods!

For the more experienced gardener the following detail may be of further guidance. You will have gathered that clematis flower either on previous seasons' ripened stems, or on stems produced during the current flowering season. The date when the clematis starts to flower is the all-important point and with this in mind pruning requirements become self-explanatory. One either leaves the old stems on the plants to obtain early flowers, or removes the old spent growth from the previous season, making way for the new growth on which flowers will be borne.

Group One. The species and cultivars that fit into this group produce their flowers on short flower stalks directly from a leaf axil bud, generally on stems produced the previous season which became ripened by the early autumn. The clematis in this group consist of the evergreen species and their cultivated forms, the *alpina* and *macropetala* types and the *montana* group. This group produce their flowers directly from the old stems and, therefore, pruning must not be carried out until all flowering has been completed.

Pruning for this group consists of removing all dead and weak stems immediately after flowering. Established plants five metres high or more are not normally pruned, especially if they are growing in trees. All stems should be tied into position or attached to their host immediately after pruning. If any of the *montana* group have become untidy, or have out-grown their allotted space, then this too is the time for any thinning out or severe pruning that may be required, again remembering to firmly attach remaining stems to the host or support. After pruning, new growth will be produced which will become ripened during the late summer and

GROUP ONE CLEMATIS

1. Flowers appear on short flower stalks directly from a leaf axil bud, generally on stems ripened the previous season.
2. After flowering, new growth is naturally produced which, in turn, will ripen before winter.
3. Flowers will appear from these buds in the following season.

GROUP THREE CLEMATIS

1. Current season's growth

GROUP TWO CLEMATIS

1. Previous season's growth
2. Current season's growth
3. Dead or weak stem that should have been removed

Flower Development

A COMPARISON OF THE THREE MAIN GROUPINGS

GROUP ONE

Cultivars:
Evergreen and Early Flowering, *alpina* and *macropetala* types, *montana*

Flowering Period:
Main batch of flowers in early spring.

Stems:
Flowers produced *generally* on stems which grew the previous year and became ripened before the autumn frosts.

Pruning New Plants:
1st year, Feb/Mar, cut back stems to 30cm. 2nd year immediately after flowering, cut all stems back to 1m.
Subequent years cut out only dead or weak stems, immediately after flowering.

Pruning Established Plants:
(those not received correct pruning in formative years so are bare at base and untidy)
Cut out dead or weak stems after flowering. Layer a stem (one a year) into the soil (see page 73) to disguise leggy stems. Treat the successful new growth as a new plant (see above).

GROUP TWO

Cultivars:
Early Large-Flowered, Double and Semi-double, Mid-season Large-flowered

Flowering Period:
Flowers late spring to autumn depending on cultivar.

Stems:
Early flowers produced on stems which grew the previous year and became ripened before the autumn frosts. Later flowers produced on current season's stems.

Pruning New Plants:
1st year, Feb/Mar, cut back stems to 30cm. 2nd year, Feb/Mar, cut back stems to 1m. Subequent years cut back all stems to a strong pair of buds, and remove dead and weak stems.

Pruning Established Plants:
(those not received correct pruning in formative years so are bare at base and untidy)
Prune only half the stems back to approx. 60cm above soil level, just above a node in early spring and just before bud break. Treat the successful new growth as a new plant (see above). Prune the second half the following year.

GROUP THREE

Cultivars:
Later Flowering Large-Flowered, *viticella*, Late-flowered species and their forms

Flowering Period:
Flowers mid summer onwards.

Stems:
Flowers on new growth – all the previous season's stems become almost useless and die naturally each winter.

Pruning New Plants:
1st year, Feb/Mar, cut back stems to 30cm. 2nd year, Feb/Mar, reduce all stems to just above the base of the previous season's stems, within 45cm of soil level.
Subsequent years, reduce all stems as in 2nd year, but within 55cm to 75cm of soil level.

Pruning Established Plants:
(those not received correct pruning in formative years so are bare at base and untidy)
Do not cut down to within 75 cm of soil as in most cases this would be fatal. Cut back to active leaf axil buds and train downwards in subsequent years.

---

produce its main crop of flowers the following spring.

Group Two. Clematis in this group produce their flowers on the old or previous season's stems and consist of the early, large-flowered cultivars, the double and semi-double and mid-season, large-flowered cultivars. The flowers are borne on single stems which vary from 10cm to 90cm in length. Whether the stems that produce the flowers are short or long, the first flowers are always produced from the previous season's ripened stems.

The observant gardener will notice the swelling leaf axil buds during the late winter onwards. These will have become fat and ready to burst into leaf in early spring and are the buds that grow during the spring months and produce the first crop of flowers from the beginning of early summer. To the experienced gardener the clematis plants will be pointing out where pruning is needed and that is just above where these strong leaf axil buds are visible.

The pruning requirements of this group consist of removing all dead and

weak stems, and shortening the remainder by 15–25cm to where a strong pair of leaf axil buds are apparent. All old leaf stalks that still remain should be removed and all remaining stems should then be tied into position immediately after pruning. The position for tying-in the stems is important and each stem should be given sufficient space where all anticipated new growth and flowers can expand to the full without overcrowding or too much overlapping of growth. When the clematis stems are being tied on to a host plant, be careful not to tie too tightly as this will only cause damage to the clematis and its host in later months, or years if metal ties are used. The pruning and tying-in of stems should be carried out during the late winter or early spring before bud break when weather permits. It is best not to prune during frosty weather both from the point of view of one's fingers and the health of the clematis!

Group Three. The third group contains the section of clematis which produce their flowers on new stems each year and in most cases each stem produces several flowers. The previous season's top growth becomes useless and dies away naturally each winter (unless the winter is a very mild one with little or no frost occurring, when the growth may remain partially alive). Therefore, all previous season's top growth must be removed to allow the current season's stems room to grow to maturity. This clean-cut, tidy up of the plant also removes any stems which may have become infected with mildew, or any other disease during the autumn, thereby giving the plant a fresh start each year.

The time for pruning is again during the later winter or early spring before bud break depending on weather conditions. The actual pruning consists of removing all old top growth down to where the strong new leaf axil buds appear, at a point just above the base of the previous season's stems, approximately within 75cm of soil level. The previous season's stems are identified by their mid-brown colouring, the older stems will be a much paler, light brown-grey colour. Many produce new stems from below the soil level each spring and this should be and is encouraged by hard pruning.

The clematis which are included within this group contain the Jackmanii types and late-flowering, large-flowered cultivars, the *viticella* group, the *texensis* group and other late flowering species, including the herbaceous types.

An impatient gardener is sometimes tempted during a very mild winter to prune this type of clematis soon after Christmas. In my experience, it is unwise to be so tempted because the strong, fat leaf axil bud may be encouraged to start growing after pruning only to be severely damaged by a sudden change in the weather. In most cases, if severe damage does not occur to these buds, the flowers are nevertheless malformed and useless; so be patient, unless your climate is a mild one. He who hesitates in this case is not lost, but is wise!

Pruning clematis in cold climates

In extremely cold climates the pruning of clematis will be very different for some types of clematis to the advice given above. Where temperatures are expected to drop annually below 10°F (–12°C) the top growth of most of the early large flowered, including the double and semi-double types, (Group Two) can be expected to be damaged to some degree. The amount of damage will depend upon the duration of the winter and whether there is snow cover or how free-draining the soil conditions are. Therefore pruning of the Group Two clematis in these countries will vary from year to year. My advice is to leave all top growth intact until the winter appears to have ended and before bud break. At this time a decision can be made, depending upon the damage caused by the winter weather, about how hard to prune back the remaining top growth. If the winter has been kind then some ripened leaf axil buds from the previous season will be remaining. If this is the case then the old top growth can be removed down to a strong pair of leaf axil buds which in turn will produce those long awaited early large flowers.

Prune above the leaf axil bud.

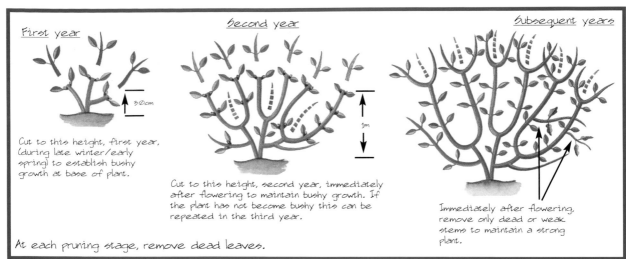

First year

Cut to this height, first year, (during late winter/early spring) to establish bushy growth at base of plant.

30cm

Second year

Cut to this height, second year, immediately after flowering to maintain bushy growth. If the plant has not become bushy this can be repeated in the third year.

1m

Subsequent years

Immediately after flowering, remove only dead or weak stems to maintain a strong plant.

At each pruning stage, remove dead leaves.

Group One

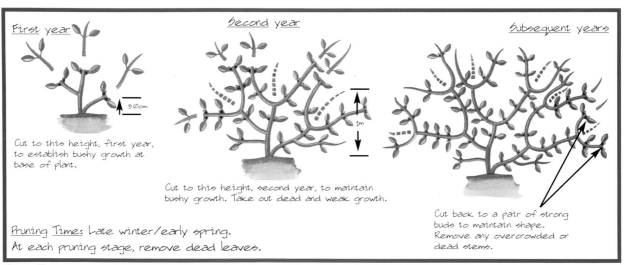

First year

Cut to this height, first year, to establish bushy growth at base of plant.

30cm

Second year

Cut to this height, second year, to maintain bushy growth. Take out dead and weak growth.

1m

Subsequent years

Cut back to a pair of strong buds to maintain shape. Remove any overcrowded or dead stems.

Pruning Time: Late winter/early spring.
At each pruning stage, remove dead leaves.

Group Two

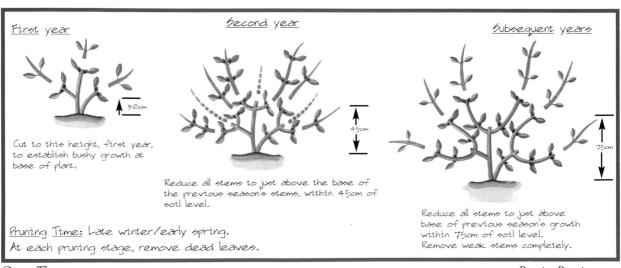

First year

Cut to this height, first year, to establish bushy growth at base of plant.

30cm

Second year

Reduce all stems to just above the base of the previous season's stems, within 45cm of soil level.

45cm

Subsequent years

Reduce all stems to just above base of previous season's growth within 75cm of soil level. Remove weak stems completely.

75cm

Pruning Time: Late winter/early spring.
At each pruning stage, remove dead leaves.

Group Three

Pruning Requirements

If the winter has been severe then the top growth will need to be cut down to soil level where new growth will appear later in the spring, resulting in late and smaller flowers that year.

The *alpina* types will not be affected by severe winters, the *montanas* may not survive (see more under the chapter on growing clematis in northern climates, page 61), and therefore at best some of the hardier forms may retain some top growth. The early large flowered types (Group Two) will be damaged as described above, the mid season and Group Three clematis can be expected to be reduced down to soil level, which is normal for those types, so their pruning requirements remain unaltered.

Pruning established clematis

Established clematis which have not received the correct pruning needed for their particular type during cultivation and have become untidy, or bare at the base, are regrettably apparent in large numbers. After reading the pruning recommendations here one must not take a pair of secateurs to a late-flowering (Group Three) type and cut it down to within 75cm of soil level as this would, in most cases, be fatal. Due to incorrect pruning such a plant would most probably not have any active leaf axil buds within 75cm of soil level. My advice for such a plant is to remove all dead and weak stems to where active leaf axil buds appear, at whatever height this may be. As new growth is produced, this may be trained downwards to give annual cover to the bare, lower parts of the clematis. This will most probably be an annual job to attain an attractive plant.

An alternative possible cure, especially with a *montana* type or a large plant of any of the *alpina* or *macropetala* types, is to layer a stem into the soil by carefully disentangling a stem from the mass of growth and slowly bending the stem down to soil level.

Layering is detailed on page 73. This will achieve fresh, healthy foliage at the base of the plant and cover up the unsightly bare base of the clematis. It is important that the successfully layered clematis should be pruned back hard in the early spring for the first two years so that a bushy base is achieved. If this practice is not possible, then the simple answer is to purchase another young plant and train it into the base of the older plant.

With an established clematis of a large-flowered cultivar (Group Two) which has become very bare at its base, there is an alternative cure that can be tried, if the plant has several stems from the base or ground level. As it would be most unwise to cut all stems down to ground level at one time in order to help regenerate the plant, it is possible to do this in stages. If the plant has several stems or even two growing from soil level, then I suggest that half of the stems are pruned down to approximately 60cm above soil level, just above a node in early spring and just before bud break. It is important that, as these stems are being removed (and some of the top growth may become damaged) care should be taken. If any stems that are to remain are damaged, these should also be cut back to just above an active leaf axil bud. If the hard pruning is successful during the first spring and new growth is achieved, then this exercise can be repeated the following spring. Any new stems that are produced from soil level, or just above, should be pinched back to again achieve a healthy base to the plant.

Another technique which is used by some clematis enthusiasts on clematis from Group Two is to prune these plants back hard (to within 45/60cm of soil level) every third year. In doing this, they regenerate the plant and get rid of any untidy tangle of old top growth. However, the large early flowers have to be given up for one year and the flowering period will

be delayed for about four to five weeks. The clematis will produce smaller flowers, but perhaps more. For the following two seasons, the plants are pruned normally by just removing dead and weak stems and shortening the remaining stems to a strong pair of leaf axil buds.

As mentioned earlier in this chapter my friends in Northern Europe, North America and Canada do not have the choice of whether or not to prune their plants of the early large-flowered cultivars (Group Two) as their severe frosts do this for them. So they can only occasionally enjoy the early, very large-flowered clematis, after a very mild winter. Instead of plants such as 'Nelly Moser', 'The President' or 'Lasurstern' flowering during late spring or early summer, they have to wait for their main flush of flowers until later in the summer. Therefore, as one can see, it is possible to experiment with the pruning of clematis as experience is gained and the flowering period can be changed.

The pruning requirements for clematis grown as container plants, for ground cover, or over heathers and other special planting schemes should be checked under those individual headings.

*Clematis alpina 'Constance',
from Pruning Group One*

Growing Clematis Through Trees Shrubs and Roses

Clematis suitable for growing over and through trees fortunately amount to quite a cross-section of types. The early and late-flowering species, which rampage to seven metres or more and their respective cultivated forms, allow us a good freedom of choice.

Evergreen trees

Most members of the pine family may be graced with the many strands and flowers of the *montana* forms. The *montanas* grow eventually up to ten metres or more and look superb when they are in full flower, appearing like a white or pink waterfall as their many vines come cascading down over the branches of the large Corsican pine, or similar sized host.

The growing of clematis underneath trees is rather more difficult than in an open position due to the dry soil conditions. However, if soil preparation as described on page 16 is carried out and adequate water is provided until the clematis becomes established, the gardener will be duly rewarded in the following years. Don't forget that establishment may take two growing seasons and in some very dry positions even three years from planting. When planting under a large tree such as a pine, a site within 30cm of the tree trunk is the most suitable position: see the diagram on page 14.

The newly produced clematis stems can then be tied into position by the use of wires until they reach into the framework of the tree's branches and attach themselves by the use of their leaf stalks (or petioles). The strength of the clematis vines will not be suffi-

The beauty of this tree is being added to by the careful training of Clematis 'Comtesse de Bouchaud' into it.

cient to cause damage to the tree.

Clematis montana and its forms were thought to be extremely winter hardy in the British Isles until the severe frosts of the early 1980s when many plants were killed completely after experiencing temperatures as low as −26°C (−15°F) in some parts of England. Work is being carried out to select the most hardy form or cultivar.

Suitable combinations

The most hardy white *montana* is the form currently being sold as *montana* f. *grandiflora*. This plant grows most successfully in Bavaria, withstanding temperatures as low as −20°C (−4°F) and still flowering freely the following spring. Obviously, it is most unusual for such cold conditions to be experienced in England and one should not be put off growing the other forms of montana. But in cold districts, it is useful to know that *montana* f. *grandiflora* will survive the most extreme winters in the British Isles. This hardy form has flowers with a diameter of 6/8cm and is a good, clear free-flowering white.

Another larger-flowered white with more rounded full flowers is *montana* 'Alexander'; this plant also has good, large leaflets. There are some very poor forms of white *montana* in cultivation which have been grown from seed so always select a good named cultivar. This also applies to the pink *montanas*. C. *montana* 'Elizabeth' is particularly pleasant with soft pink flowers which are a little gappy but have a lovely scent. Slightly deeper coloured and stronger scented is 'Pink Perfection'. 'Odorata', an old form I found in Sweden, has a delightful vanilla scent and is also pale pink. Two more recently introduced montanas are 'Freda' and 'Mayleen'. *Clematis montana* 'Freda' has extremely dark pinkish-red flowers and most attractive dark bronze foliage. *Clematis montana* 'Mayleen' has pale pink flowers which are produced extremely freely and have the strongest scent of any of the *montana* cultivars that I grow. *Clematis montana* 'Tetrarose' has most attractive bronze foliage as well but additional attractions are the large serrated leaves. The flowers of this cultivar are possibly the largest of the pink montana types, being a good 5/7cm in diameter. C. *montana* var. *rubens* 'Picton's Variety' is possibly the most compact growing of all the pink *montanas*, growing only to about 6 metres.

Clematis chrysocoma (white and pink forms) and *vedrariensis* 'Highdown' are both closely related to the *montanas* but are not so vigorous, growing only to about 6/7 metres. All of the *montana* types flower during late spring and early summer and grow, with the above exceptions, up to 8/10 metres or sometimes more in very favourable conditions. The two latter clematis and *montana* var. *rubens* 'Picton's Variety' are suitable for growing through evergreens such as a large *thuya* or lawson's cypress and its many ornamental forms, green, golden or even the various grey-foliaged forms, all of which offer a perfect background to the pink flowers of the clematis.

When the *montana* types are being grown in large evergreens and the initial hard pruning has been carried out to encourage the plant to become bushy at its base, they can be then left unpruned. If any stems become detached from the branches of the tree then the ideal time for pruning and tying-in of the stems is immediately after flowering. This will then give the plant time to make new growth so that the following year's crop of flowers is not unduly affected by pruning.

Evergreen hollies can be graced with the tumbling blossoms of the later flowering species and small-flowered cultivars. *Clematis flammula*, a starry, white-flowered scented species from Southern Europe, looks magnificent when in full flower: the stems appear to be clothed with flowers and show up well against the dark green foliage of a holly. Many of the other pale-flowered clematis such as the white 'Huldine', with its freely produced 6cm diameter flowers, also look well growing through an open-branched holly.

The yellow variegated holly trees lend themselves also to show up the flowers of the colourful *viticella* cultivars. Among the attractive range of *viticella* clematis, 'Abundance' wine red, 'Kermesina' deep red, 'Royal Velours' velvet purple, 'Etoile Violette' purple with prominent yellow centre and the similar coloured 'Blue Belle' which has larger flowers, are some of the best for growing in association with the lighter coloured variegated hollies.

Due to the form of a holly tree and the importance of its appearance during the winter months, a late-flowering species or cultivar should be used, so that the larger part of the spent clematis growth can be removed during the later autumn allowing the holly to look tidy during the winter months with the final pruning of the clematis being completed during the early spring before bud break.

Yews, especially the large open trees, not the carefully trimmed ones, also lend themselves to the rampaging species. C. *potanini* var. *fargesii*, a fine white clematis with 3cm diameter flowers which are produced in abundance from early summer onwards, looks delightful when it has reached a height of six metres on a yew and is in full flower. The delicate, nodding white flowers of *viticella* 'Alba Luxurians' look splendid against the dark background of the old English yew. This clematis is slightly unusual due to each tepal having a green tip, the centre being a deep purple black and the flowers semi-nodding in form. As one can imagine from the description, it is a little out of the ordinary and well worth a position in a large garden. Due to the important appearance of the yew during the winter months, the lengthy stems of the late-flowering clematis may be reduced in late autumn, with the final and correct pruning being carried out during early spring before bud break. The *montana* family, I feel, should not be grown over yews, purely because of the untidiness of the old growth during the winter months, and this is why I recommend the later-flowering species and cultivars for appearance and ease of cultivation. As well as the white-flowering species *potanini* var. *fargesii*, *viticella* 'Alba Luxurians' both previously mentioned, 'Huldine' and *flammula* are also white and lend themselves to be grown and flower against the dark foliage of a large yew. Our native clematis commonly known as "old man's beard" or "traveller's joy", *Clematis vitalba*, also needs a dark background to display its many thousands of creamy white flowers. The masses of silky seed heads from which the common names have obviously derived look best when the stems, which grow to nine metres, can be allowed to clamber up a tree.

Clematis serratifolia, which is similar to the more commonly grown *tibetana* and its forms, also looks well on a dark background. This vigorous species from Korea grows to six metres in height and has pale yellow flowers which are nodding and composed of four tepals with a central tuft of deep purple-red anthers. The flowers are produced from late summer until the first autumn frosts. *C. terniflora*, again white, needs the framework of a large tree to display its hawthorn scented blossoms. This species which attains six metres of growth needs a hot sunny position to flower well in the British Isles. Until several years ago it had been known as *C. paniculata* and in more recent years *maximowicziana*, however it has been corrected once more to *terniflora*. In the United States of America the plant is still incorrectly called *paniculata*.

For the garden which contains only a moderate sized conifer, yew or similar type of evergreen tree, some of the mid-season large-flowered cultivars and the later-flowering cultivars

Clematis 'Proteus' can have double, semi-double or single flowers.

may be successfully used to add colour and a variation to the white-flowered species that need at least a ten metre high tree. Of the mid-season flowering clematis, the blues such as 'Violet Charm' mid blue, 'Belle Nantaise' pale lavender blue, 'Blue Ravine' pale blue, 'Peveril Pearl' very pale lavender with rosy highlights and the large-flowered whites 'Marie Boisselot' and 'Henryi' may be utilised. The pruning requirements of these large-flowered cultivars, if grown in such a situation, need to be changed and they can be pruned fairly hard in the early spring before bud break to encourage plenty of new growth. Some old stems to the height of one-and-a-half to two metres should be left to produce the early flowers. The hard pruned stems will then produce flowers later, during the summer months. The late, large-flowered cultivars such as 'Comtesse de Bouchaud' and 'Hagley Hybrid', both of which are pink-mauve, and the semi-nodding, pale blue flowers of

'Perle d'Azur', may also be used to add colour and interest to the dark background of a yew which will display their pale coloured flowers to best advantage.

Pruning clematis on evergreen trees

The gardener unaccustomed to growing clematis through other plants, shrubs and trees may be slightly worried and concerned about damage to the host when pruning is to be carried out. As mentioned earlier, clematis stems attach themselves by the leaf stalk (petiole) but this attachment is slowly reduced when the winter months approach. After several frosts the foliage of the deciduous clematis starts to decay and falls from the plant, leaving the leaf stalk loosely attached to the host. By early winter, when I recommend that the Group Three types have their top growth reduced to leave the yew, conifers or other evergreen in a tidy state for the remaining winter months, the leaf stalks will come away from their support without causing damage. There is no need to use a pair of garden steps to reach the top growth of the clematis which may have reached a height of five metres or so. The severed stems may be gently, but firmly, tugged from the tree or shrub, causing virtually no damage, and then burnt. The final and correct pruning may then be carried out during early spring before bud break as weather conditions permit. This double type of pruning when the top growth is reduced to one-and-a-half metres or so in early winter is, in fact, an advantage. It ensures that a good selection of active leaf axil buds is available when final pruning is carried out in early spring, and will keep the plant bushy and well furnished at its base.

Deciduous trees

Whereas the soft and hardwood evergreens lend themselves beautifully to hosting clematis, regrettably the deciduous hardwoods, such as oak, elm, sycamore, planes, limes, etc., do not, due to the nature of their structure. Also, in my opinion, the appearance of these elegant and graceful trees would be spoilt with climbers of any type clambering about their branches.

However, deciduous trees the size and shape of the flowering cherry, *Sorbus*, lilac, *Laburnum*, *Robinia*, even old cherry, damson, pear or apple trees that have passed their best regarding fruiting, but are retained in the garden because of their character and shapes, are ideal. Any one of these types of tree may be successfully used to host the stems of a clematis giving the necessary support and allowing the flowers to be shown to their best advantage. The erect-growing *Prunus* 'Amanogawa' which grows in a slender column needs the addition of another plant to give it colour during the period when its flowers

Clematis viticella 'Polish Spirit' is a very free-flowering cultivar.

have passed their best. The pale pink flowers of 'Comtesse de Bouchaud' look refreshing as they trail from this *Prunus* at two metres high and further upwards as the season progresses. The late-flowering species and late-flowering, large-flowered cultivars are the most successful for smallish, deciduous trees. The reason for this is again because I like a garden, however natural it may be, to appear under control during the winter months. Therefore the late-flowering clematis may be provisionally tied up during early winter with final pruning being carried out at the correct time in early spring as described under the Evergreen Tree section.

Selecting and positioning your clematis

The selection of species or cultivar must depend upon individual taste but choice of flower colour, foliage association and the actual tree being used should all be taken into account.

However, there are several additional points that need to be considered. The first is that the host tree should be studied regarding the position of the clematis planting site because the clematis branches will naturally grow towards the sun on the lightest side of a small tree where they will then flower. Therefore, on a small tree some training of stems during the early part of each summer is required, so that one can then select the flower-ing position, because if left to nature the vines will grow into the lightest area which may not be the most effec-tive place.

On a large tree, where the total circumference is much greater, the position where the clematis will flower can be more easily pre-deter-mined due to the fact that the stems will mostly grow and flower on the side they are planted. When consider-ing the flowering position of a clema-tis it is important, therefore, to consider both the height and type of a host tree and the height of the clema-tis. As a guide, the ultimate height of the late, large-flowered cultivars varies between two-and-a-half and four metres, and the species vary from about three metres in height.

The density and colour of foliage of the tree is another important factor. For instance, if the foliage is pale coloured as with *Pyrus salicifolia* 'Pendula' (the silver-foliaged weeping pear), a purple clematis such as the free-flowering *viticella* 'Etoile Violette' or the ever popular 'Jackmanii Superba' may be used, but if the foliage is very dark, as with a pear or thickly branched apple tree, one must choose a pale-flowered clematis such as 'Comtesse de Bouchaud', 'Huldine' or the pale-flowered *viticella* cultivars 'Minuet', 'Margot Koster', 'Little Nell' or 'Alba Luxurians'.

As a further guideline, the follow-ing planting association, using a medium-sized deciduous tree and one of the late-flowering large or small-flowered cultivars, may be considered. The autumn-flowering cherry *Prunus subhirtella* 'Autumnalis Rosea' is an ideal, open-branched, lightly foliaged tree giving the correct support and framework, where one of the *viticella* cultivars such as 'Abundance', 'Madame Julia Correvon', 'Kermesina' can be shown to great advantage. In this instance one is adding colour to the tree during mid to late summer,

*Clematis **Anna Louise**™ 'Evithree'® growing with pale blue ceanothus.*

but the main clematis top growth is removed before the cherry commences flowering.

The golden foliage of *Robinia pseudoacacia* 'Frisia' is an absolute must to display the purple flowers of either *viticella* 'Etoile Violette' which produces masses of medium-sized flowers, the newer larger-flowered *viti-cella* 'Polish Spirit' with purple-blue flowers or, alternatively, 'Gipsy Queen' with large, deep purple flowers; these clematis flower from mid summer onwards. To enhance the dense foliage of a *Laburnum*, one should choose a free-flowering clema-tis such as the *viticella* cultivars: 'Margot Koster' with pale rosy-red flowers, or 'Minuet' with delightful white flowers veined throughout with

mauve. The contrast of the purple flowers of 'Jackmanii Superba', or the carmine-red flowers of 'Ville de Lyon', will also give much-needed colour to a *Laburnum* tree from mid summer until early autumn. *Sorbus cashmiriana*, with its fern-like foliage, is an ideal host for late-flowering cultivars like 'Star of India', a very free-flowering deep purple-blue, and the rosy purple flowers of 'Victoria'. The clematis add colour and interest to the *Sorbus* after its flowering time and before the glis-tening white berries in the autumn.

Large shrubs

Both evergreen and deciduous shrubs lend themselves to hosting clematis. The list of suitable hosts in this section could be nearly endless. I must, therefore, leave the final decisions of combination to the imaginative gardener; but again there are some guidelines that may assist with the choice of host and the selection of the correct type of clematis.

The large-flowered cultivar and tall-growing species rhododendrons lend themselves perfectly to the support of the twining stems of a clematis. The mid-season, large-flowered cultivars need such a host so that their natural, free growing, open framework of stems can spread themselves, distributing their very large open flowers widely over their support. This group of clematis produces flowers on the previous season's and current season's stems and this must be remembered when the clematis is being trained during the growing season. Some of the best mid-season, large-flowered cultivars which grow successfully with rhodo-

dendrons are the lavender-blue of 'Masquerade' or the slightly paler blue 'Belle Nantaise'. The superb 'Marie Boisselot' with large white blooms or the pale lavender of 'Peveril Pearl' all lend themselves well to this plant association. 'Violet Charm' with its pale blue flowers and red anthers looks equally good when grown with pink flowering *syringa* species.

Medium sized shrubs

A selection of early, large-flowered cultivars, double, and semi-double cultivars may also be used to grow through rhododendrons or a similar type of shrub which is not more than five metres high. The proposed host should not have an open framework of branches where wind can blow directly through the host, causing distress to the clematis vines by detaching them from their support. Due to the flowering habit of this

selection of clematis and the closeness of each flower to one another and the shortness of the flowering stems, the host needs to be compact. *Rhododendron, cotoneasters,* (the large-leafed densely branched types) large *pyracanthas, escallonias,* and free-standing deciduous shrubs including established Japanese maples, *Cercidiphyllum, Cercis, Cotinus* and *Cytisus battandieri* are all suitable hosts.

Of the early large-flowered clematis, a selection of the following cultivars will give a good range of colours: 'Barbara Jackman', blue with petunia bars, 'Bees' Jubilee' mauve pink with deeper central bar, 'Elsa Späth' mid-blue, 'Ken Donson' deep blue overlapping tepals, 'Lasurstern' clear blue, 'Masquerade' mauvish blue with pointed tepals, 'Nelly Moser' mauve-pink, 'Niobe' red, 'Pink Champagne' syn. 'Kakio' purplish-pink, 'The President' purple-blue and 'William

Clematis **Vino**™ *'Poulvo'*® *is ideal for growing with climbing roses.*

Clematis 'Royalty' produces double, semi-double and single flowers.

formed rosette-like flowers on the old wood in spring and single flowers on current season's wood, later in the summer. An old cultivar that should not be omitted is 'Belle of Woking' with slightly mauve-white, fully double flowers and, of course, the newer semi-double 'Royalty' with rich purple-mauve flowers and yellow anthers in the spring and single flowers during the later summer months.

Possibly the best of all the double clematis is our 1994 introduction **Arctic Queen**™ 'Evitwo'® which produces double white flowers most freely, both from old or new growth. The amount of flower this new cultivar produces is staggering from early summer until the end of the autumn months.

The outstanding 1998 introduction, **Josephine**™ 'Evijohill'®, with its dramatically different flowers, looks marvellous with grey or purple foliaged shrubs. Its lilac-pink flowers have many pointed tepals that create a pom-pom effect when the flower is fully open. Mid-season cultivars include 'King Edward VII' puce-violet, 'Marie Boisselot' white, 'Maureen' purple and 'Serenata' rich purple. If desired a selection of late-flowering cultivars can also be used to give a longer and more varied flowering period through the season: cultivars such as 'Ascotiensis' blue, 'Ernest Markham' red, 'Gipsy Queen' rich purple, 'Jackmanii Superba' purple-blue, 'Madame Edouard André' dusky red, 'Perle d'Azur' pale blue and 'Ville de Lyon' carmine red. The *viticella* cultivars may also be added to the list of possible varieties to choose from, giving a good variation of habit and flowering periods for the gardener with a large garden who is in need of a continuity of flowers from late spring until early autumn.

Plant associations that I have found most satisfying include the use of *Pyracantha rogersiana* 'Flava', whose

Kennett' pale blue. Of the less common cultivars, 'Gillian Blades', which is white with a hint of pale blue, has beautiful wavy edges to the tepals which are pale blue, making a very full flower, also with creamy white anthers, and is particularly long flowering. 'Fireworks' lives up to its name with a full display of colourful flowers of purple and red with red anthers.

Cultivars of more recent introduction from our nursery which should be mentioned here are **Anna Louise**™ 'Evithree'® named after my second daughter which has striking and dramatically-coloured violet flowers with a contrasting red/purple bar and red anthers, **Royal Velvet**™ 'Evifour'® which has a very free-flowering habit throughout the summer months with

rich velvet purple flowers and red anthers, **Sugar Candy**™ 'Evione'® has large pale pink flowers with a darker central stripe and yellow anthers, and the 1995 introduction **Liberation**™ 'Evifive'® which has deep reddish pink flowers also with a darker central band and yellow anthers. **Blue Moon**™ 'Evirin'® which was introduced in 1997, has white flowers suffused with pale lilac, red anthers and wavy edges to the eight tepals.

Double and semi-double cultivars which may be used include 'Countess of Lovelace' pale lavender with pointed tepals, 'Proteus' mauve, 'Vyvyan Pennell' purple-mauve and the semi-doubles 'Lady Caroline Nevill' pale lavender and 'Mrs George Jackman' white. Another semi-double white is 'Sylvia Denny', with tightly

bright green leaves are a pleasant background to the plummy-purple flowers of 'Kathleen Wheeler'. The purple foliage of *Acer palmatum* 'Atropurpureum' is a superb foil to the pink flowers of 'John Warren', or the pale lavender flowers of 'Mrs Cholmondeley'. *Cotinus* 'Foliis Purpureis' or *Cotinus* 'Royal Purple', with their outstanding purple foliage, display the flowers of 'Nelly Moser' mauve-pink, 'Perle d'Azur' pale blue and the white flowers of 'Mrs George Jackman' to great advantage. The choice of *Cytisus battandieri* and 'Victoria' is a delightful combination when the silver-grey leaves of the *Cytisus* are looking their best and the yellow pineapple-like flowers of the shrub and the rosy purple flowers of the clematis are all performing at the same time. The association of 'Marie Boisselot' and the grey-green foliage of *Cotoneaster franchetti* is also very desirable. And, of course, a delightful combination can be achieved by growing the free-flowering 'Niobe' through the various forms of variegated dogwood (*Cornus*): the combination of its rich red flowers with the delicate variegated foliage and red stems of the host is a must.

Shorter-growing shrubs

Compact, more densely branched shrubs such as some varieties of *Pyracantha*, compact forms of *Cotoneaster*, evergreen *Ceanothus*, *Camellia*, *Aucuba*, which may be free-standing or wall-trained, are all satisfactory hosts for the early large-flowered cultivars and the double cultivars which, due to the size and density of their flowers, require protection from the wind. The selection of clematis in this case needs thought: one must take into consideration the flowering time of the host; one must decide if the clematis should flower before, with, or after the host has flowered; and the colour of the flower and foliage of both host and clematis are vitally impor-

The deep red flowers of Clematis viticella 'Kermesina' contrast well with this conifer.

tant considerations.

A selection of clematis for compact, lower-growing evergreen shrubs includes the early, large-flowered cultivars such as 'Asao' pale pink, 'Pink Champagne' (syn. 'Kakio') deep mauve-pink, 'Barbara Dibley' petunia red, 'Bees' Jubilee' pink mauve striped, 'Corona' purplish pink, 'Dawn' pearly white, 'Edith' white with a prominent red centre, 'H. F. Young' Wedgwood blue, 'Horn of Plenty' mauve, 'Lady Londesborough' pale blue, 'Lady Northcliffe' clear blue, 'Miss Bateman' white, 'Mrs N. Thompson' blue with red stripes, 'Mrs P. B. Truax' periwinkle blue. The newer cultivars which have a compact free flowering habit are 'Guernsey Cream' creamy yellow, **Anna Louise**™ 'Evithree'® violet with contrasting red/purple bar, **Royal Velvet**™ 'Evifour'® rich velvet purple and 'Masquerade' lavender rosy-blue. Two older cultivars now becoming more widely available are 'Snow Queen' white with rosy to blue tints and 'Ruby

Glow' with glowing ruby red tepals.

Double and semi-doubles which flower from early summer onwards include 'Countess of Lovelace' pale blue, 'Duchess of Edinburgh' white, 'Vyvyan Pennell' purple-mauve and the semi-double 'Daniel Deronda' purple-blue and the outstanding **Arctic Queen**™ 'Evitwo'® with clear white flowers.

A selection of some of the later-flowering cultivars which flower from mid summer onwards may also be used to give an added colour range and continuity of flowering. Some of the most satisfactory are: 'Ascotiensis' bright blue, 'Comtesse de Bouchaud' pink-mauve, 'Gipsy Queen' deep purple, 'Hagley Hybrid' rosy pink, 'Madame Edouard André' dusky red, 'Perle d'Azur' pale blue, 'Victoria' rosy purple and 'Ville de Lyon' carmine red, and the striking new cultivars **Liberation**™ 'Evifive'® deep pinkish red and **Sugar Candy**™ 'Evione'® pink-striped. *Texensis* cultivars 'Duchess of Albany' cherry-pink,

Here Clematis 'Niobe' associates well with this low growing jasmine.

'Gravetye Beauty' ruby-red and the fascinating new **Petit Faucon**™ 'Evisix'® with its semi-nodding deep blue flowers also extend the selection of shapes, sizes and colour range from which the discerning gardener can choose.

The low-growing shrubs which do not attain a height greater than two metres force the clematis to display their flowers below this height. Thus one does not have to look upwards to the sky to view the flowers at close quarters as with some of the previous plant association recommendations.

Cotoneaster microphyllus, grown as a free standing shrub, rarely attains more that just over a metre in height, making an ideal host plant on which the *texensis* cultivars 'Duchess of Albany', 'Gravetye Beauty' and 'Sir Trevor Lawrence' can display the miniature tulip-like flowers which need to be looked directly into to gain the full pleasure of their unusual shape. The slightly grey foliage of *Cotoneaster buxifolius vellaeus* is a splendid foil to enhance the pale pearly-white flowers of 'Dawn' which are produced from early summer onwards. Both cotoneasters have a low arching habit and dainty leaves which cluster around the stems, giving an interesting contrast in foliage shape and colour, as well as emphasising the obvious attraction of the clematis flowers. Plants of *Ceanothus* 'Autumnal Blue' are occasionally grown as a free-standing shrub in mild localities, and the glossy green evergreen leaves plus the powder-blue flowers which appear from early summer onwards offer the possibility of hosting several clematis, all of which can either flower before the ceanothus or with it. 'Mrs N. Thompson', 'Vyvyan Pennell', **Liberation**™ 'Evifive'® or **Sugar Candy**™ 'Evione'® all early summer

flowering, will also produce their second crop of flowers while the ceanothus is flowering. The semi-double 'Daniel Deronda' will produce its deep purple-blue flowers before and while the host is flowering. The mauve-pink flowers of 'Comtesse de Bouchaud' are produced while the ceanothus is in flower, giving an even greater combination of colours.

The grey foliage of *Brachyglottis greyi* presents itself beautifully to show off the contrasting colour of early-flowering cultivars such as 'H. F. Young', Wedgwood blue, the white flowers of **Arctic Queen**™ 'Evitwo'®, the rosy mauve of 'Hagley Hybrid' or even the dusky red flower of 'Madame Edouard André'.

Another marvellous combination using a grey foliage shrub and a clematis is a planting association between *Phlomis fruticosa*, with its thick grey leaves and pale yellow flowers, and the old clematis cultivar 'Madame Grangé', with its deep plummy-purple flowers. This super old plant usually has six tepals that are somewhat boat shaped, never opening fully, which gives it additional charm and interest. A similar colour combination is to use the new cultivar **Royal Velvet**™ 'Evifour'® which will give the same effect but earlier in the summer or to use **Blue Moon**™ 'Evirin'® with its white flowers suffused with lilac blue, would look rather sophisticated.

Clematis in association with roses

The use of clematis with wall-trained, pillar or climbing roses on pergolas or archways can be most effective, each offering its companion either support or colour when the other is not in flower, thus gaining maximum effect from a small area of one's garden. The association can also be carried through to the garden where roses are grown as free-standing shrubs.

Every year the use of roses as shrubs is increasing. The old-fashioned shrub roses include the splendid Gallicas, Albas, Damasks, Centifolia and Moss roses, all of which are easily placed in a modern garden either in groups, hedges or as specimen plants. The hybrid teas, and to a slightly lesser extent the cluster roses, are more difficult to place in a garden if one wants to get away from the typical way of planting roses like soldiers in rows.

The delightful "old roses" give us colour, form and scent, but regrettably have a limited flowering period as compared with the cluster roses, although their framework of branches and foliage gives us the ideal support for the large-flowered clematis. Due to the pruning requirement of the roses the late large-flowering cultivars are the best, thus avoiding the conflict of clematis stems to remain and rose stem to be removed. The gardener who knows his old roses may well use some of the early large-flowered cultivars through some of the roses which require less pruning.

Once again, if the experienced gardener requires to use a particular clematis cultivar because of the colour of the flowers, then the early-flowering cultivar may be pruned harder than generally recommended with the result that the flowering period will be delayed, the large early flowers being lost, but the desired result of colour association will be achieved. The Jackmanii types such as 'Ascotiensis', 'Comtesse de Bouchaud', 'Gipsy Queen', 'Hagley Hybrid', 'Jackmanii Superba', 'Madame Edouard André', 'Perle d'Azur', 'Star of India' and 'Victoria' offer various shades from blue, pink, red and purple, all of which blend well with the flowers of the shrub roses. Some of the newer introductions such as 'Pink Fantasy' peachy pink, 'Prince Charles' mauve blue, and 'Rhapsody' sapphire blue, all lend themselves very well indeed to growing with roses of any type, due to their free-flowering habit.

These plants grouped together make a striking combination. They are Clematis 'Gypsy Queen' and Clematis 'Bees' Jubilee' with Abutilon striatum.

Another successful association that I've seen was achieved by underplanting a bed of pink and red cluster roses with 'Jackmanii' and *integrifolia* var. *integrifolia*. The large purple flowers of 'Jackmanii' look fascinating popping up through the roses. The nodding mid-blue flowers of the herbaceous *integrifolia* var. *integrifolia* also look fun scrambling around just beneath the roses or just clambering up into the lower stems. The pink *integrifolia* 'Rosea' or the rarer but beautifully scented white *integrifolia* 'Alba' would also blend well with the correct shades of the cluster roses.

And so the combinations and planting can go on, creating a picture in one's mind one year, planting the next and hopefully seeing the realisation the following year and for many years to come. With a little imagination and careful selection of both host and clematis, and good cultivation, one can achieve most satisfactory results.

Using Clematis as Ground Cover

Only a few clematis are capable of complete ground cover, in the sense of the true meaning of the word, which is "to cover and smother the ground". When clematis species are found growing in the wild they scramble around at ground level and eventually locate a suitable support on to which they grow and climb, to possibly flop back down the support or climb even higher. From this description one can assume that many of the clematis species are suitable for ground cover, if this term is used loosely.

The smothering types which will sprawl around until a suitable support comes within reach are as follows: *cirrhosa* var. *balearica* and the newly introduced *cirrhosa* 'Freckles' with its larger, deeper spotted flowers. Both of these are evergreen clematis and native of the Mediterranean regions, but regrettably are not completely winter hardy. If they are to be used as successful ground cover, they need an almost frost-free position. They both produce creamy white nodding flowers which have purple blotches on the inside of each tepal.

All of the *alpina* and *macropetala* group naturally scramble and smother at ground level. *Alpina*, a charming European species, has given rise to

The cultivar Clematis 'Dawn' creeps at ground level.

many cultivars, all of which have single, four-tepalled nodding flowers. Some of the most free flowering are 'Columbine' (pale blue), 'Pamela Jackman' (deep blue), 'Frankie' (mid-blue with blue markings on the inner petaloid stamens), 'Helsingborg' (deep purple-blue), 'Willy' (pink) and 'Frances Rivis'. This latter is the largest flowered *alpina* with long, slightly twisted pale blue tepals.

Two of the recently introduced *alpinas*, 'Constance' and 'Pink Flamingo' have almost double flowers. These two with ruby red and pink flowers are a most welcomed addition to this useful group. 'Pink Flamingo' is perhaps the most exciting with pale pink flowers with darker red vein to the base of the tepal, it also has a good long flowering period. Another *alpina* of recent introduction is 'Blue Dancer' with similar coloured flowers to 'Frances Rivis', its tepals are narrower and longer. 'Foxy', a pale pink sport of 'Frankie', is extremely free-flowering and certainly worth growing.

Macropetala, which is a native of China, with lavender blue semi-double flowers, has also more recently given rise to a range of cultivars such as 'Blue Bird' (mauve-blue), 'Rosy O'Grady' (pink-mauve), 'Lagoon' (deep violet blue), 'Jan Lindmark' (purple), 'White Wings' (white) and 'Pauline' (very large mid-blue flowers). The older 'White Moth' (white) and 'Markham's Pink', also an old cultivar, are some of the best of this superb range which look delightful scrambling around at ground level, especially if there is a rock or some form of support to give the plant added height and another dimension. The *alpina* and *macropetala* types will give a cover of approximately three square metres.

Clematis montana and all of its family make a very dense ground cover giving a cover of approximately eight square metres after three years. The reader will recall that this

Late summer flowers of Clematis alpina 'Foxy' with seed heads from spring flowering.

rampaging species can vary from white to various shades of pink, and can climb up to ten metres in a tree, therefore, give your *montana* plant sufficient space to develop and keep it trained after each season's flowers have faded.

Of the later-flowering species which can give very good ground cover, *serratifolia* pale yellow, *tibetana* var. *vernayi* and *tangutica* var. *tangutica*, both yellow, are all capable of growing each year to give a ground cover of approximately six square metres. *Clematis akebioides*, a plant

similar to *tangutica* in habit but with the added attraction of having glaucous, finely-cut foliage, is a little more out of the ordinary. Its flowers are smaller than those of *tangutica* var. *tangutica* but are produced in masses and are creamy on the inside of the tepal and slightly bronzy on the outside, giving the plant an interesting colour mix, especially when in full flower. The medium-sized white flowers of 'Huldine' look refreshing against its deep coloured foliage when allowed to scramble at ground level, and is capable of covering five to six

Clematis viticella cultivars on winter-flowering heathers.

square metres annually.

The small-flowered cultivar × *jouiniana* and its early-flowering form 'Praecox' are among the best smothering clematis because their foliage is coarse and their leaves large, which means they give total ground cover. This cultivar between *vitalba* ("old man's beard") and *heracleifolia* var. *davidiana* produces delightful, soft lavender hyacinth-like flowers from mid summer onwards. Its range is only about three square metres but it is ideal for ground cover and to scramble over short tree stumps that are in need of camouflage.

As one would imagine, *vitalba* makes a superb ground cover plant.

This species, like all the others in this section, is shown to advantage if allowed to scramble over some form of vertical support. If no natural support in the form of a rock or natural bank, or rise or fall in the ground level is available, then something should be added. Stout branches of a hardwood tree may be placed in the site, with one end placed into the soil to a depth of 60cm or so to give stability. The branch may be cut to a desired size or shape, and then placed into the soil at an angle to give yet further interest.

From reading several old books on gardening I find that clematis, and in most cases the large-flowered cultivars, were grown on such supports as

I've just described. The mind boggles at the thought of seeing clematis grown in this way, as permanent bedding plants in specially selected beds with the added interest of shaped tree branches to give the necessary height. The later, large-flowered cultivars would be best, I feel, because the beds could then be tidied up each spring, when all the previous season's growth could be removed. Mid-season large-flowered cultivars could also be used in this type of scheme and the plants would not come to much harm if they received hard pruning similar to the late flowerers. Their presence would add variety in flower shape, flowering time and colour range.

Personally I feel that a flower border given over entirely to clematis would be rather uninteresting during the winter months, and here the use of several different types of evergreen shrubs would be invaluable. The ones I have in mind are *Cistus × corbariensis* and × *cyprius* 'Silver Pink', *Corokia cotoneaster*, *cotoneaster* varieties like *adpressus* and *buxifolius vellaeus*, any of the broom family as they can look splendid with clematis vines trailing through them especially if there is a breeze, *Cytisus albus* 'Burkwoodii', *nigricans*, × *praecox* and *purpureus*.

Other plants to consider are the evergreen *Daphne retusa*, *Erica mediterranea* 'Superba' a tree heather and *eucalyptus* which are pollarded back each spring and kept as bushes. *Eucalyptus gunnii* makes a splendid winter foliage plant. Also try *Genista lydia* and the evergreen hardy hebes, especially the grey foliaged ones. At the front of such a proposed border the rock roses (*Helianthemum*) can be grown, making a marvellous carpet for odd clematis vines to trail on. *Senecios*, lavenders and the evergreen *Prunus laurocerasus* 'Otto Luyken' could also be used. I feel this gives a sufficient range to choose from which would provide a variety of foliage form, shape of bush and colour of leaf and flower.

Some of the shrubs which I have recommended for the special clematis border planting idea can also be used as individual hosts for some less rampaging late-flowered species and their cultivars. The American species *viorna*, *pitcheri*, and *texensis* have fascinating urn or pitcher-shaped flowers. The gorgeous *texensis* cultivars 'Duchess of Albany' pink, 'Gravetye Beauty' glowing red and 'Princess Diana' pink, have delightful little flowers that give the impression of being miniature tulips. The flowers of 'Gravetye Beauty' open slightly more than those of 'Duchess of Albany'. *Clematis* 'Durandii', a large-flowered non-clinging cultivar with deep indigo-blue flowers with a cream coloured centre, needs the support of a low-growing shrub where its stems can just flop and ramble about. The elegant double flowers of *viticella* 'Purpurea Plena Elegans' show up very well when grown over the rounded form of *Hebe rakaiensis* (*subalpina*) which has fresh, apple-green foliage. A semi-herbaceous × *aromatica* looks most interesting when it is allowed to scramble over a grey foliage shrub, dispersing its small starry purple flowers over its host. As you can see, the options available to the gardener with imagination and time to plant such planting schemes is vast, if not inexhaustible.

Clematis and heathers

One of the most successful plant associations that I have become aware of is the use of the *viticella* cultivars to grow over winter-flowering heathers. A large bed of winter-flowering heathers is splendid from late winter onwards;

Clematis texensis 'Etoile Rose' *has a vigorous nature and here has been left to scramble happily over this wall.*

This old cultivar, Clematis 'Jackmanii Rubra' looks striking growing amongst any grey foliaged plant.

but the flowers of the heathers then fade away, leaving a rather uninteresting carpet of fresh green until the next flowering season. With the use of *viticella* cultivars, the green carpet can be transformed into a very pretty patchwork of colours from mid summer until the early autumn months.

Clematis viticella itself varies in the wild from differing shades of bluish-mauve to white. It was introduced in the 16th century from Central Europe to British gardens and has since given rise to many splendid small-flowered cultivars. The ones most worthy of garden value and for the purpose of planting over heather are as follows: 'Abundance', deep pinky-red, 'Alba Luxurians', a fascinating white form with tepals that reflex, most tepals having a green tip, 'Etoile Violette' which has 7cm diameter deep violet

flowers with contrasting creamy anthers, 'Little Nell' with creamy white flowers with overtones of mauve, 'Madame Julia Correvon', with wine-red flowers – a rather gappy flower, each tepal twisting and recurving at the tip – 'Margot Koster', another gappy-type flower, with deep mauve-pink flowers, 'Minuet' which produces an abundance of semi-nodding flowers that have a white background and mauve veins at the margins, 'Royal Velours' whose flowers are so deep in colour they need the light background of one of the golden foliage heathers to show the flowers to best effect – the flower is a full round shape and the tepals are a deep velvety purple – 'Kermesina' with masses of deep wine-red flowers, and lastly the delightful veined flowers of 'Venosa Violacea' which are the

largest of this group, reaching about 7–8cm in diameter with the boat-shaped tepals veined throughout with purple on a white background that give the flower a fascinating appearance. The newish deep purple-blue 'Polish Spirit' is a stunning plant being raised in Poland by Brother Stefan Franczak. This plant is perhaps a little too vigorous for small young heather beds but is ideal for growing up into conifers or large shrubs on the fringe of heathers, allowing a few strands of its delightful flowers to flop over the heathers.

The method for planting the *viticellas* amongst heathers is quite straightforward. The clematis need to be planted at approximately one and a half metres apart and it may be necessary for a heather plant to be removed from an established bed. Soil preparation as described on page 16 should be carried out unless the heather bed was well prepared before planting. If a heather bed which has only been planted for a few months, is to be used, it is advisable to allow the heathers twelve to eighteen months to become established so that the clematis will not swamp the young heathers.

The clematis, when grown over heathers in this manner, should be pruned back hard in early winter to allow the heathers to start their flowering at the correct time and also to prevent rain-soaked clematis leaves sagging onto the heathers causing harm to their foliage and possibly spoiling their flowers. The amount of clematis growth during the summer months is not sufficient to cause harm and the heathers will not become spoilt or smothered. Due to the earlier than normal pruning of the clematis,

new growth may appear early the following year if the winter is at all mild. If this is the case, and there are also mice present in the heather border, damage may occur, and the prevention method suggested under the Pest and Diseases section on page 76 should be carried out.

The *viticella* cultivars are equally successful when used to enhance the flowers of the summer-flowering heathers; and in addition to the *viticellas*, the *texensis* cultivars and 'Durandii' may also be used to give many interesting flower and colour combinations.

The fascinating **Petit Faucon**™ 'Evisix'® with its semi-nodding deep royal blue flowers, yellow anthers and its non-clinging habit to about one metre, also looks very very dramatic when grown through heathers.

Clematis and annuals

Late, large-flowered cultivars can also be used to scramble through and over many of the summer-flowering, annual bedding plants. *Clematis* 'Jackmanii Superba' looks splendid planted with deep purple-red asters, and the effect is even better if several other taller-growing plants such as woolly-leafed *Helichrysum petiolare* or the grey-foliaged *senecios* are dot-planted amongst the asters. The range of bedding plants is vast; and I suggest that anyone wishing to try out this particular idea should spend a little time during one summer planning such a border with annuals and the permanent planting of clematis, and looking in other gardens for ideas of plant and colour associations.

Clematis 'Durandii' scrambling at ground level.

Clematis in Containers and in the Conservatory

Unfortunately not all gardeners are able to cultivate and grow clematis in the natural manner, with the root system established into good garden soil and the plant able to grow through a suitable host plant. The exciting fact is that some clematis can be grown successfully in a container. Frustrated gardeners who are limited in garden space, people with only small patio gardens, or even those who have to put up with the ever-increasing spread of concrete, can take advantage of growing clematis in this way.

Clematis grown in containers have many uses. They can brighten up dull parts of a concrete yard area, along the walls of buildings that are surrounded by hard stone, or by concrete pathways where no natural soil or flower beds can be prepared for planting. The conservatory, cold glasshouse, or even a naturally well-lit living room or garden room lend themselves to the cultivation of certain varieties of clematis for pot or container culture. A 30cm diameter container with an early large-flowered clematis in full flower, with perhaps twenty or thirty blooms, will make an everlasting impression on any gardener's mind, and tempt even the

There is no need for elaborate pots or support constructions, if you feel these are beyond you. The most inexperienced of gardeners can grow clematis as this Clematis × cartmanii 'Joe' demonstrates. This cultivar can grow quite large with a wonderful profusion of flowers.

anti-clematis person into attempting to repeat such a spectacle.

The correct choice of clematis is the most important factor but the correct size and type of container and the right mixture of compost are also vital. Other details such as watering, feeding, training and the general health of the container-grown clematis need careful attention. Such detail and patience is rewarded each spring when the clematis starts into new growth, followed by those handsome, large, colourful flowers.

Choosing your clematis

The choice of clematis species or cultivar is, I feel, the most important decision to be made. This problem is made easier by the fact that the only choice, with a few exceptions, is between those varieties within the early-flowering group. If a container-grown clematis is required for a small patio, sun lounge, garden room or balcony area, the plant should be of a naturally compact, bushy habit and produce its flowers on the old wood, or the previous season's ripened stems. The *alpina* and *macropetala* cultivars, the evergreen types, with the exception of *armandii*, are delightful "pot clematis", but the period of flower is limited. If area and space are not a problem and several different plants are to be grown to flower over an extended period, then the small-flowered types should be tried.

If space is limited and only one or two plants can be grown, then one should rely on the early large-flowered cultivars. Within this range there is great choice: in colour, flower form and to some extent flowering period. Some of the first ones to flower in this group are **Anna Louise**™ 'Evithree'®, 'Asao', **Blue Moon**™ 'Evirin'®, 'Dawn', 'Edith', 'Edouard Desfossé', 'Etoile de Paris', 'Masquerade', 'Miss Bateman', 'Mrs P. B. Truax', 'Pink Champagne' syn. 'Kakio', **Royal Velvet**™ 'Evifour'® and 'Ruby Glow'.

Clematis 'Ruby Glow' has a compact, free flowering habit, ideal for container growing.

These are all very compact in their growth and flowering habit and produce their main flowering flush in late spring or early summer. They are ideal to train and make an absolutely glorious, if perhaps oversized, pot plant for a small area, producing twenty to thirty flowers on a plant only 1m high in a container with a 30–45cm diameter. The slightly later-flowering types in this group are perhaps the most rewarding. Varieties similar to 'Nelly Moser' and 'The President', which flower during early summer, are also followed by a further crop of flowers during the late summer months.

The *montana* group and some of the vigorous, tall-growing species such as *tangutica*, *tibetana*, *serratifolia* and *rehderiana* are, unfortunately, far too vigorous to be grown in a container successfully.

Flowering of these types would be rewarding during the first few years when the compost in the container is fresh and contains the correct balance of foods; but when top growth reaches five to seven metres and the root system more or less fills the container, the gardener would be forever watering and feeding the plant.

The late-flowering, large-flowered cultivars can be grown successfully although they do not make the same type of compact plant as the early large-flowered group. This group, which includes the famous *Clematis* 'Jackmanii' and its many forms, flowers on the new growth only; therefore, all the previous season's top growth is removed in the early spring allowing new growth to be made. This new growth needs careful training and one should remember that the flowers are produced at the end of each stem generally after two-and-a-half metres of growth has been accomplished. Despite the additional work involved,

this group, plus the small flowered cultivars of the *viticella group*, are worth the extra effort of container growing.

Choosing and preparing your container

The material from which the container is made is important. The use of plastic tubs or plastic containers should be avoided, the main reason being that the container does not insulate the clematis roots from the heat of summer or from the cold of winter. As mentioned earlier in the book, clematis prefer a cool root run and, therefore, a plant growing in a thin walled plastic tub in an exposed sunny situation would be caused great distress in a hot summer, even with extra watering. In winter, such a container would again expose the clematis root system to very little or almost no insulation against severe

frosts. However, there is still a great range of containers to choose from: for example, old half beer barrels, stone, earthenware or some of the more pleasant, modern designed wooden containers.

The size of the container is, however, important. It should be not less than 45cm deep with a diameter of 30–40cm, larger if available, and there should be sufficient drainage holes. With a container of this size there should be at least three drainage holes, each with a 5cm diameter, or five to six holes with a 2cm diameter.

Pebbles or broken pottery must be placed over the drainage holes to a depth of about 6cm; small stones and pea gravel scattered over the pebbles will also assist drainage and avoid the clogging of the holes with compost after watering, or by earth-worms. Make sure that if the bottom surface of the container sits flat on the standing

Clematis florida **Pistachio**™ *'Evirida'*® *is a new cultivar ideal to be grown with evergreen wall-grown shrubs or in a conservatory.*

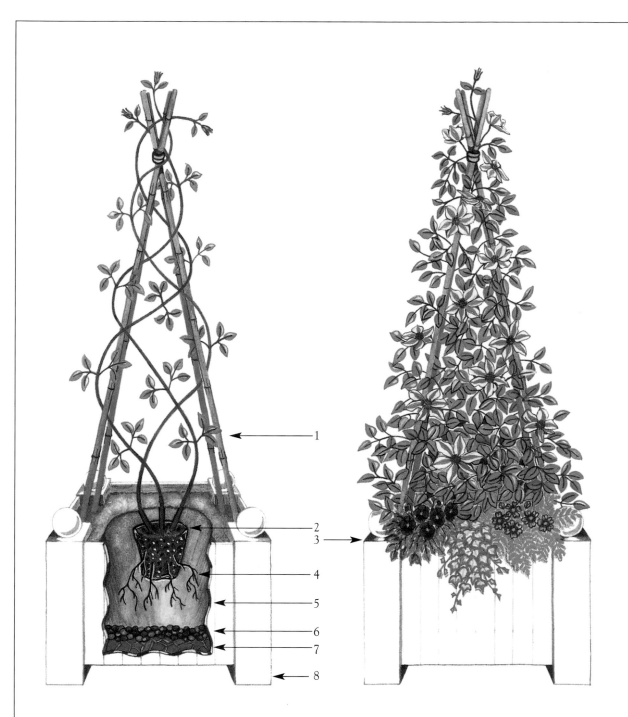

1. Canes tied wigwam fashion to provide support for clematis
2. Root crown buried 5cm below soil surface
3. Soil surface covered with low growing plants providing shade for root system
4. Main base roots slightly loosened
5. John Innes Potting Compost No.3
6. Layer of small stones or pea gravel to assist drainage
7. Pebbles or broken pottery placed over drainage holes to a depth of 6cm
8. Container raised off ground to prevent drainage holes blocking

Planting and training your container grown clematis

CLEMATIS SUITABLE FOR CONTAINER CULTURE

Winter flowering or early spring under glass
(glasshouse or conservatory conditions)
cirrhosa 'Freckles'
cirrhosa var. *balearica*
florida 'Plena'
florida 'Sieboldii'
paniculata

Late spring flowering
alpina 'Columbine'
alpina 'Constance'
alpina 'Frankie'
alpina 'Foxy'
alpina 'Pink Flamingo'
alpina 'White Columbine'
alpina var. *ochotensis* 'Frances Rivis'
macropetala var. *macropetala*
macropetala 'Jan Lindmark'
macropetala 'Lagoon'
macropetala 'Markham's Pink'
macropetala 'Pauline'

Later spring flowering
Alabast™ 'Poulala'®
Anna Louise™ 'Evithree'®
'Asao'
'Bees' Jubilee'
Blue Moon™ 'Evirin'®
'Burma Star'
'Carnaby'
'Corona'
'Dawn'
'Edith'
'Edouard Desfossé'
'Elsa Späth'
'Etoile de Paris'
'Fireworks'

'Fujimusume'
'Gillian Blades'
'Guernsey Cream'
'Haku Ookan'
'H. F. Young
'Horn of Plenty'
Liberation™ 'Evifive'®
'Masquerade'
'Miss Bateman'
'Moonlight'
'Mrs P. B. Truax'
'Pink Champagne' ('Kakio')
RoyalVelvet™ 'Evifour'®
'Ruby Glow'
'Scartho Gem'
'Silver Moon'
'Souvenir du Capitaine Thuilleaux'
Vivienne 'Beth Currie'

Early summer flowering
Arctic Queen™ 'Evitwo'®
'Belle of Woking'
'Countess of Lovelace'
'Daniel Deronda'
'Duchess of Edinburgh'
'Dr. Ruppel'
florida Pistachio™ 'Evirida'®
florida 'Plena'
florida 'Sieboldii'
'John Warren'
Josephine™ 'Evijohill'®
'Kathleen Wheeler'
'Kiri Te Kanawa'
'Lady Northcliffe'
'Lasurstern'
'Louise Rowe'
'Marie Boisselot'
'Mrs Cholmondeley'
'Mrs George Jackman'

'Mrs N. Thompson'
'Multiblue'
'Nelly Moser'
'Niobe'
'Proteus'
'Richard Pennell'
'Rouge Cardinal'
'Royalty'
'Snow Queen'
'Sunset'
'The President'
'Twilight'
'Veronica's Choice'
Vino™ 'Poulvo'®
'Vyvyan Pennell'
'Walter Pennell'
'William Kennet'

Summer flowering
'Ascotiensis'
'Dorothy Walton'
'General Sikorski'
'Hagley Hybrid'
'John Huxtable'
'Madame Edouard André'
'Perrin's Pride'
Petit Faucon™ 'Evisix'®
'Pink Fantasy'
'Prince Charles'
'Rhapsody'
'Violet Charm'
viticella 'Betty Corning'
viticella 'Kermesina'
viticella 'Madame Julia Correvon'
viticella 'Purpurea Plena Elegans'
viticella 'Royal Velours'
viticella 'Venosa Violacea'

area, stones are placed underneath the container to lift it off the ground: this will greatly assist drainage and avoid blockage and water saturation of the container during prolonged rain or snow periods in the winter months.

In my experience, the only suitable compost to put into the container is that prepared under the John Innes formula, and John Innes potting soil No. 3 should be used. The No. 3 mixture is of extra strength, Nos. 1 and 2 being far too weak for long-term pot culture. This compost is readily available from many garden centres and garden shops. There are many other composts offered for sale, including loam-free mixtures which contain a percentage of peat and grit or sand. They are most useful for short-term growing of crops, especially annuals, but are of no use for long-term pot culture where they require far too much attention to maintain a correct nutrient balance and where liquid feeding also becomes difficult if the compost dries out. When using

John Innes potting compost, the top 6–8cm of soil should be carefully replaced each spring using the same John Innes No. 3 potting compost. At this time, attention should also be paid to the drainage holes, ensuring they are not blocked.

Planting your container

After the correct choice of clematis has been made, a suitable container prepared and filled to within 6cm of the rim, planting may now commence. Planting in a container is, or can be described as, re-potting and may be carried out at any time of the year, although obviously the points mentioned under the section dealing with garden planting should still be considered. Summer planted clematis will require more watering in order to achieve good and quick root establishment.

The plant, still in its original pot, should be plunged into a bucket of water and left to soak for at least 15 to 20 minutes. Then carefully remove the pot from the root ball, loosening the outer, bottom-most roots slightly, as previously described on page 18. Bury the root crown at least 6–8cm below the soil surface of the container as this will help the plant's survival rate if damage should occur at any stage in the plant's lifetime by animals, or when pruning or re-potting is being carried out.

In exposed, cold locations where heavy snowfalls or wet winters can be expected or, even worse, where low temperatures can be expected without snow cover, then it is advisable to take clematis growing in containers into a well-lit garage or out-building. This will avoid the root system being exposed unnecessarily to severe conditions and will prevent it from being damaged by long periods of severe frost or becoming sodden with water. This will also avoid damage to the ripened top growth from the previous growing season, as one needs

Here Clematis Josephine*™ 'Evijohill'® has been trained to almost cover this Flower Belle.*

to retain as much as possible to attain the largest possible amount of flower for the next flowering season. My friends in northern parts of the U.S.A., Canada and Northern Europe take their container-grown clematis under cover each winter so they can achieve a good, well clothed flowering plant for the following spring. If this has to be done, then obviously it is important that any clematis grown in a container should have its support attached to the container or be supported by a frame which is anchored into the compost: it would become a little difficult to remove part of the house wall each autumn to take inside with the clematis attached!

*Clematis **Blue Moon**™ 'Evirin'® is ideal for container growing.*

Pruning and training the container-grown clematis

Pruning and training of a pot or container-grown clematis follows the same basic principles as for a free-growing plant, but careful pruning and training are more important if the best looking container plant is to be produced. The first spring after planting (depending on weather conditions), the clematis must be pruned hard with all stems previously produced being removed down to 24cm above soil level. This severe action is necessary to encourage several new stems to be produced at a low level, thus forming the basic framework of the plant for the future.

The pruning cut should be made just above a strong leaf axil bud, or better still, a pair of buds. These buds will be visible during early spring. When new growth commences and three pairs of leaves or nodes have been formed, the growing tip must then be removed. This will encourage the production of two or three new shoots from each stem, at the stage when the new growth is still soft and green and before the unapparent leaf axil buds have become at all woody.

The new growth subsequently produced should be carefully trained and tied into position on to the various supports that have been provided (more about the choice of supports later). If possible, train the stems to grow almost horizontally in a circular manner around the support framework, commencing as low as you can.

After the hard work in the spring, no further pruning is required until the following year and you may allow your clematis the freedom of flowering. I assure you, if you have been strong-minded enough to carry out this pruning the first spring after planting, you will be justly rewarded. The many plants which I have prepared for our exhibits at recent Chelsea Flower Shows were all treated in this way.

Support

The selection of a support or framework for the container grown clematis needs consideration. If the clematis is to be grown against a wall or through another host plant, then the support is already decided, but an auxiliary cane should be led from the container to the main support or strong branch of the host. For the free-standing container plant there are many and varied metal and wooden supports for plants available on the market. Simple cane or stick supports may also be placed inside the container and tied together at the top, wigwam fashion. Metal rods coated with a polythene or plastic film and bent into various hoops or pyramid shapes are all equally interesting and worthy of experiment. The climbing supports made of wood and shown on page 47 are very useful clematis supports, this particular one is called a Flower Belle.

Looking after your container grown clematis

Throughout the growing season, from spring until late summer, container-grown clematis will need regular attention such as the tying-in of new growth. It is essential that the new growth is tied in as it is produced and this will only take a few minutes per week.

Watering is the most time consuming job, with each 45cm clematis container requiring the equivalent of 4.5 litres (a gallon) per day during the dry spring and summer weather. A guide to water requirement can be tested by disturbing the compost a few centimetres below the surface. If it is moist or sticks to the finger, the plant will not require water on that day; but if the compost is like dust, then water is necessary. Do not give the plant small amounts of water at a time since this will only keep the surface moist and the area where the roots are at the bottom of the container will remain dry. If watering is restricted, this will reduce the top growth, which will in turn limit the number of flowers produced. It is most important to remember that sufficient water is a must with the cultivars which are expected to carry a second batch of flowers during mid summer. Basically, watering reaches a peak during mid-summer when water will be required each day, unless there has been rain. Less water will be required as autumn approaches and stopped altogether by mid autumn, except for the very occasional watering necessary to stop the soil from becoming dust dry. Liquid fertilizer can be incorporated during watering but should never be applied to dry soil: water first and then use. If liquid feed is taken up by roots which have been starved of water, the root hairs will be damaged causing unwanted harm to your clematis. There are many liquid feeds offered on the market and any reliable brand-name product is suitable. A well balanced feed with equal parts of Nitrogen and Potash is best for the growing season. As previously mentioned in the section dealing with "Annual Feeding and Mulching of Established Plants" (page 20), the liquid feeding of container-grown clematis should also stop prior to flowering. It is therefore advisable to stop feeding as soon as the most prominent flower bud is about the size of a pea. The continuation of clear water is vital and, in fact, should be attended to very closely. If the container-grown plant should become at all dry at this time, the successful flowering of the plant could be in severe doubt.

As soon as the last flowers fade away, the use of liquid feed becomes very important again so that healthy new growth can be made to produce the next crop of flowers in the season. Liquid feeding should be discontinued by late summer because the amount of new growth made from that time will be naturally reduced and it is important that growth should be hardened and ripened for the following season, especially with the early-flowering cultivars which flower on the previous season's ripened stems.

Pruning in subsequent years

When all foliage has died, and possibly fallen to the ground during the winter, and the fat leaf axil buds are visible during the later winter months and early spring, pruning and training can commence.

Canes tied wigwam fashion are the easiest framework to make to encourage the clematis to climb upwards.

All varieties which flower before early summer belonging to Group Two should be carefully pruned. The amount of pruning required must be judged by experience. However, as a guide to the beginner, all dead and weak stems should be reduced to the point where strong, swollen leaf axil buds are present. The "fat" buds are the ones which will produce the first large flowers during late spring and early summer. The selected stems that remain after pruning should be tied into place and great care must be taken not to knock off any buds or crack any of the stems as they are being trained. The exact position in which the stems are tied must be left to the gardener and the individual framework that is being used. However, if the stems are tied in an almost horizontal position, new growth will be produced and grow vertically, giving a good cover to the lower part of the supports. The stems of the large-flowered cultivars should be spaced far enough from each other so that each swollen leaf axil bud will develop and hopefully produce a flower which will have sufficient space to grow without overcrowding. The decision as to how many stems to leave or remove will be made easier by experience. It is easy to be greedy and leave too many stems which will cause reduced flower size.

If the later-flowering types are being used, the pruning for this is the same as for the open ground or garden varieties of the same group: simply remove all top growth down to just above the swollen buds, which normally are in the vicinity of the base of the previous season's growth. As new growth appears, this should be tied into position before it becomes over 30cm long. These stems also can be trained in a semi-horizontal position. If this growth is merely allowed to grow straight to the top of the support, the plant will look less interesting and you will be disappointed

CLEMATIS FOR THE CONSERVATORY

Winter and spring flowering
× *cartmanii* 'Joe'
cirrhosa 'Freckles'
cirrhosa var. *balearica*
paniculata

Late spring flowering
alpina 'Columbine'
alpina 'Constance'
alpina 'Foxy'
alpina 'Frankie'
alpina 'Pink Flamingo'
alpina 'White Columbine'
macropetala 'Lagoon'

Later spring flowering
Anna Louise™ 'Evithree'®
'Asao'
'Bees' Jubilee'
Blue Moon™ 'Evirin'®
'Burma Star'
'Dawn'
'Dr Ruppel'
'Edith'
'Edouard Desfossé'
'Etoile de Paris'
'Fujimusume'
'Gillian Blades'
'Guernsey Cream'
'H. F. Young'

'Lady Northcliffe'
'Lasurstern'
'Masquerade'
'Miss Bateman'
'Mrs N. Thompson'
Royal Velvet™ 'Evifour'®
'Ruby Glow'
'Silver Moon'
'Souvenir du Capitaine Thuilleaux'
'Twilight'

Early summer flowering
Arctic Queen™ 'Evitwo'®
Josephine™ 'Evijohill'®
'Louise Rowe'
'Mrs George Jackman'
'Multiblue'
'Royalty'
'Veronica's Choice'

Summer flowering
florida Pistachio™ 'Evirida'®
florida 'Plena'
florida 'Sieboldii'
Petit Faucon™ 'Evisix'®
'Pink Fantasy'
'Prince Charles'
'Rhapsody'
tangutica 'Helios'
viticella 'Betty Corning'

with the result. Pruning of Group One clematis can be carried out after flowering by removing any dead and weak stems.

The pruning and training sounds most complicated when written in this manner but do not be put off container-grown clematis. Admittedly the work is time consuming, but it is definitely worth the effort and time taken. The cold fingers experienced during the winter and early spring months, the backache etc., will be truly rewarded when the plants are in full flower, and the pain will be forgotten.

With experience gained over two or three years, the enthusiastic

gardener will soon start to experiment with different varieties to grow, or the shapes and style of framework used, and many fine "pot plants" will be produced for the conservatory, garden room, patio or balcony.

CLEMATIS IN THE CONSERVATORY
If a conservatory, garden room or cold glasshouse is available, a succession of flowering "pot plants" may be produced by careful selection of species, their forms and cultivars. These can be forced or retarded and brought into this extended garden or living-room. In Victorian times, the culture of clematis in this way for the

house, conservatory or show bench was well practised. Today, we have an even larger selection to choose from which includes the slightly tender evergreen types that will provide foliage and flower during the winter months. The range of cultivars being raised by crossing some of the New Zealand species is to be looked out for. C. × *cartmanii* 'Joe' is one which produces a dense mat of white flowers a little over an inch wide. As I write this section I have a plant of this outstanding clematis in my office in a 3 litre pot on a 60cm high wire, dome-shaped frame, it has over 400 flowers!!! and has been flowering already for two weeks with another two weeks I guess to flower. The plant would last even longer in a cooler room or glasshouse. However, ones that are more readily available at present are the good forms of the charming *cirrhosa* var. *cirrhosa*, *cirrhosa* var. *balearica* with finely cut slightly bronze foliage, and the newer *cirrhosa* 'Freckles', a plant I introduced in 1989. C. *cirrhosa* 'Freckles' has the largest flowers of any of the *cirrhosa* forms; the leaves, too, are larger than the species. The foliage of all these plants is evergreen.

The flowers of 'Freckles' are borne from the previous season's ripened stems during late autumn and early winter, with the occasional summer flower. The flowers of all *cirrhosa* types are nodding and comprise four tepals. They are cream inside and are covered in pink-red blotches. C. *cirrhosa* 'Freckles' has flowers 4–5cm in depth which are slightly scented. The tepals recurve a little at the edges, revealing the stunning colour inside the flower. Its flowers have the most intense colour and are almost totally covered with blotches. The other forms of *cirrhosa* flower from just after Christmas under glass.

Two good New Zealand clematis to look out for are *paniculata*, with white tepals, and *forsteri*. The flowers of *paniculata* are produced, as with all

The evergreen Clematis cirrhosa 'Freckles' will provide foliage and flowers in the conservatory during the early winter months.

winter-flowering clematis, from the previous season's ripened stems. This species varies; therefore, a good broad-flowered form should be selected. The best have flowers 4–5cm across with lovely pink anthers, which are produced in late winter. As mentioned in an earlier chapter, the best winter-flowering clematis for strong scent is *forsteri* which produces small creamy-green flowers in great abundance. When this plant is in full flower in late winter or early spring, the lemon verbena scent from the flowers is almost overpowering. C. *australis* is similar but has more finely cut foliage, which is most attractive, but not so strong a scent.

The winter-flowering, small-flowered clematis can be followed by the earliest of the early, large-flowered cultivars which would flower during early spring under cold glasshouse conditions. Again, these produce their flowers from the previous season's ripened stems. Some of the earliest to flower are 'Asao' pale pink, 'Pink Champagne' syn. 'Kakio' deep pink-mauve, 'Dawn' very delicate pale pink, 'Miss Bateman' white with red anthers, 'Wada's Primrose' cream and 'Lady Londesborough' pale blue. These early, large-flowered cultivars are sometimes flowering just after the charming, nodding *Aquilegia*, or Granny's Bonnet, like *alpina* and *macropetala* types. The *alpinas* have single flowers with four tepals and come in shades of blue, white, red and mauve. The *macropetalas* have double flowers and are available in similar shades. Some of the freest flowering *alpina* types are *alpina* 'Columbine', 'Constance', 'Foxy', 'Frankie', 'Helsingborg', 'Pink Flamingo' and 'White Columbine'. Some of the outstanding *macropetala* types are *macropetala* var. *macropetala*, 'Jan Lindmark', 'Markham's Pink', 'Pauline' and 'White Moth'.

The next main flowering batch are the slightly later, large-flowered cultivars such as 'Nelly Moser' pink striped, 'The President' deep purple-blue, 'Lasurstern' blue, 'Bees' Jubilee' pink striped, 'Niobe' deep red, 'Horn of Plenty' mauve, 'Guernsey Cream' cream and 'Fireworks' a new stunning mauve-blue with red stripes. Of more recent introduction are **Anna Louise**™ 'Evithree'® petunia-red with contrasting purple/ red bars, **Royal Velvet**™ 'Evifour'® reddish velvet and 'Masquerade' lavender blue. The doubles such as 'Royalty' and 'Vyvyan Pennell' both mauve-purple, 'Proteus' mauve-pink, **Arctic Queen**™ 'Evitwo'® white, 'Daniel Deronda' semi-double purple-blue, can all be used to extend the early part of the summer. Any of the above mentioned types, except the evergreens, can either be forced on by using a little extra gentle heat or be retarded by placing the plants in a shaded north-facing position, out of direct sunshine.

Some of the newer introductions that are also proving their worth for both spring/summer and repeat flowering in the autumn are 'Sunset' deep scarlet red, **Liberation**™ 'Evifive'® reddish pink, the pink striped **Sugar Candy**™ 'Evione'®, 'Pink Fantasy' peachy pink, 'Prince Charles' mauve blue, and 'Rhapsody' sapphire blue.

The later-flowering Jackmanii types, such as 'Comtesse de Bouchaud' pink, 'John Huxtable' white, 'Hagley Hybrid' pink-mauve or the free-flowering *viticella* cultivars, such as 'Etoile Violette' purple, 'Madame Julia Correvon' red, 'Alba Luxurians' white with green tips to the tepals, 'Polish

Clematis florida 'Sieboldii' is at home both in the conservatory and in the garden.

Spirit' purple and 'Venosa Violacea' white with purple veining can be used and respond to forcing. The middle season large-flowered cultivars such as 'Marie Boisselot' white, 'Will Goodwin' pale blue and 'W. E. Gladstone' blue, are almost too vigorous to grow in a container for the conservatory; however, if enough space exists and a container up to 60/70cm diameter with a depth of 60 cm can be used, and a 150 cm high trellis can be supported by the container, then these extra large-flowered cultivars can be used to flower from early summer until early winter. The flowers may become smaller as the season continues and the flower colour may change slightly, due to lower light levels, but they are still worthy of time and effort and give much added interest late in the autumn months.

Before I conclude this section I must mention – or rave about – the extraordinary long-flowering duo of *C. florida* 'Sieboldii' and its double white form, 'Plena'. Given good growing conditions in a container, these

two (which were introduced from Japan as long ago as 1837) will flower almost continuously from early spring to early winter when growing under glasshouse conditions in England while in Guernsey in our glasshouse they are hardly ever out of flower. They are not so rampant as the large-flowered cultivars but are most colourful. *C. florida* 'Sieboldii' has creamy white tepals and a stunning purple boss of petaloid stamens; the flowers can be up to 8cm across and are produced in great abundance. 'Plena' has a fully double white flower, about the same size. As light levels decrease, the white tepals become more creamy-green in colour and, by winter, almost green in normal, cold glasshouse conditions.

As you will have realised by now, it is possible to grow clematis in containers and have them flowering throughout the year in a conservatory, garden room or cold glasshouse, if care is given to cultivation and the selection of species or cultivars.

Clematis on Walls and Other Structures

Clematis are useful plants to grace a wide range of structures. Some vigorous types are most successful for covering unsightly walls, while others can be used to give additional interest and colour to other plants and climbers growing over pergolas, archways and fences.

Walls

You will have gathered, by now, that I prefer plants to grow in a natural situation, as far as possible. The placing of a clematis plant to grow against a blank wall goes very much against my way of gardening. However, I accept the point that in some cases this may be necessary and must be done.

If a clematis is to be grown against a wall there are a few important things to remember. Firstly, the soil preparation should be good and the plant should be positioned at least 30cm away from the base of the wall, as shown in the diagram on page 14. Secondly, the plant should be pruned hard in its first two years to encourage it to produce a good low framework of branches and the stems may be trained in horizontal manner and then allowed to grow upwards. This pruning and training early in the plant's life will provide a well-formed

This Clematis viticella 'Venosa Violacea' would have looked much more attractive growing through another wall-trained shrub.

plant and avoid that all too familiar sight of one straight clematis stem and then a bird's nest collection of growth about two metres above ground level.

Several factors will influence the choice of plant: the area which is to be covered, the ultimate height which the clematis may reach, and the flower colour in relation to the colour of the background, avoiding, for example, pale flower colours on sunny, south walls. The shading of the clematis root system and lower part of the plant is a must on a dry, sunny, south or south-west facing wall. The use of low growing shrubs such as lavenders, helianthemums, hebes, heather etc., will give the necessary shade to the root systems.

Artificial supports

The selection of support must be given thought and there are numerous types of trellis and plastic-covered wire available in various shapes, sizes and colours. The choice must be left to the gardener to select the one most in keeping with the wall or style of house. The total height and weight of the clematis foliage which the support will have to carry must also be taken into account. On outbuildings ordinary 7cm wide mesh chicken wire or sheep netting for the vigorous species is practical, but this would not be the case if the site were adjacent to an important door entrance.

The clematis vines need to be able to reach a support in one form or another every 8–10cm, either horizontally or vertically; and to bridge the gap between soil level and the first strong support, a cane should be firmly attached to the wall support and the first growths of the clematis tied to the cane.

Using wall-trained shrubs as supports

The use of a wall-trained shrub has many advantages because the framework of the host branches or stems allows the clematis to grow naturally and very little training is necessary. Obviously the host needs to be tied against the wall but elaborate trellis and wire supports are unnecessary as most wall trained shrubs can be tied to a masonry nail placed into the wall at the required spacings. Most host plants should be given two years to become established before a clematis is planted to grow through them.

The choice of host seems almost endless but some of the most satisfactory are the evergreens including *Azara, Camellia, Ceanothus, Garrya elliptica, Magnolia grandiflora* and *Pyracantha*. Deciduous shrubs such as *Jasminum, Wisteria, Buddleia, Chaenomeles*, roses, *Cotoneaster horizontalis, Cytisus battandieri*, etc., also give sufficient support.

The selection of host and clematis is an easy one and the possible combinations are extensive. The clematis can be chosen to flower at the same time, before or after its host. All of the less vigorous species and all of the large-flowered cultivars whether early, mid or late season flowering, may be used.

The clematis that need the support of wall-trained shrubs include the evergreen, early-flowering species and their cultivars that produce the gigantic-

Clematis 'Henryi', a reliable old cultivar.

Clematis on Walls and Other Structures

Clematis alpina 'Ruby' is providing cover for this old brick shed wall.

Clematis on Walls and Other Structures

sized flowers. They dislike a windy position and need the protection of a wall site, as do some of the less vigorous species, for instance *florida* 'Sieboldii' and *florida* 'Plena'. On a north facing wall the *alpina* and *macropetala* types look delightful when growing through *Chaenomeles*. 'Nelly Moser', 'Dawn', 'Bee's Jubilee' and 'Lincoln Star', with their flowers in various shades of pink, brighten up a north-facing wall and look well when grown through camellias or pyracanthas.

Climbing and wall-trained roses give the clematis vines plenty of support when climbing through their branching stems. Here, the choice of clematis and rose is important so that the pruning requirements of the rose and clematis will be basically the same. Life can be very difficult for the clematis stems and damage may be caused if the rose needs severe pruning annually and the clematis does not, but this can be avoided with a little thought. The point made in the last sentence obviously applies to all of the other wall shrubs used. Thought must also be given to the ultimate height of both clematis and host: to grow a *montana* or *tangutica* over a *Ceanothus* or *Pyracantha* would mean suffocation for the unfortunate host within four years.

Posts

The thought of using a clematis to clothe an individual bare post hurts me about as much as planting a clematis to grow against a blank wall. If posts are in need of being furnished with a shrub, I believe that both for appearance's sake and for the plant's wellbeing a clematis grown in association with another shrub, such as a pillar or climbing rose, makes a far better proposition.

If, however, space is only available for a clematis, some varieties are better than others. The late-flowering, large-flowered cultivars are best. 'Hagley Hybrid' which produces masses of

pink flowers from early summer onwards, and 'Madame Edouard André' with her dusky-red flowers, also from early summer onwards, may be used alone to give a colourful display. Of the slightly newer clematis, two Polish cultivars, 'Niobe' and 'General Sikorski', are also most useful for this purpose, both being vigorous and free-flowering. 'Niobe' has very deep red flowers with contrasting yellow anthers, and 'General Sikorski' has large rounded mid-blue flowers with creamy centres.

If a more rampageous clematis is required, the *montana* types or the late-flowering species such as *tangutica*

and *tibetana*, with their yellow lantern-like flowers, may be used; but they will need more attention, especially when they are in full flower and foliage. The stems will need tying-in to avoid damage during any strong winds or gales, and the supporting post will need to be of a hardwood with the bottom sunk at least 65cm into the soil and also firmly anchored in a concrete base. Two slightly less vigorous clematis from this group, that can also be grown up posts, are *tibetana* ssp. *vernayi* 'L & S' 13342 with thick tepals and delicately cut glaucous foliage, and *akebioides* (described earlier) which also has attractive glaucous

Clematis macropetala var. macropetala is growing here on a north wall with the support of Chaenomeles.

Clematis 'Jackmanii' shown to its full glory in association with another wall-trained shrub.

(ivy), *Jasminum*, *Parthenocissus* (virginia creeper) *Passiflora* and *Vitis* (the ornamental and fruiting vines) all give a great variation of flower, foliage and form which is complemented by the clematis.

The *montana* family may be used on a large pergola or archway, and the stems and foliage will eventually give a great deal of cover and shade on the top of the framework. The flowers will generally be near the growing tip of the plants (from the previous season's ripened stems). The supports and posts of the pergola will also need clothing and the *alpina*, *macropetala* and early large-flowered cultivars will fulfil this role, producing their flowers from late spring until early summer. The mid-season and late large-flowered cultivars will give flowers from early summer onwards and also give more height with growth reaching the top of the support posts at two-and-a-half metres and then trailing along to the top to cascade back down again covered in flowers. Hopefully, the large-flowered cultivars will also give a second crop of flowers during late summer and early autumn. The planning needs careful thought so that the archway or pergola does not become too heavily leaden with foliage, causing structural damage: stout support posts and rigid cross bars should be used.

The pruning requirements of both host and clematis must also be observed. If any of the early large-flowered clematis are used because of the choice of colour, they may be pruned hard; the early large flowers would be fewer but a crop of flowers would be produced on the new growth six weeks or so later than normal.

The kinking and twisting of stems, when handling, pruning, or training other shrubs on the framework, should be avoided if at all possible, as this may cause partial damage to the vine later in the year when the foliage and flowers need every bit of moisture and sap

foliage and is covered in a mass of small flowers which are bronze-yellow on the back of the tepal.

Pergolas and archways
Rustic pergolas and archways add charm and character to any garden and offer yet another place where the enthusiastic clematis grower may cultivate and grow a range of clematis.

A pergola or archway given over entirely to clematis is not to be desired; but if other climbers and shrubs are used in association with clematis then the effect is tremendous, giving colour, flower and foliage for most months of the year. Climbing and pillar roses, *Lonicera* (honeysuckle), *Wisteria*, *Akebia*, *Actinidia*, *Ampelopsis*, *Chaenomeles*, *Hedera*

The deep purple-blue flowers of Clematis 'Daniel Deronda' climb through a wall-trained robinia.

the stems can provide. Clematis of different varieties but similar flowering period may be grown together but it is advisable to choose plants with the same pruning requirements. Life becomes increasingly tedious if one attempts to disentangle the growth and stems of a *montana* and a late large-flowered cultivar from one another during pruning. One's fingers become cold, one's temper is tested, one's eyes become rather crossed and the clematis stems become damaged. Unless you are even-tempered and have good eyesight, be warned!

Fences

A fence made of chain-link, wire, or wood is one of the coldest places to ask any self-respecting plant to grow through or over. Therefore, only the strong-growing species or small-flowered cultivar clematis can be considered. The height of the fence is not important since a clematis will climb until there is no further vertical support, at which point its vines will fall back naturally. So if the fence is one or even three metres in height, the choice of clematis is left open between the strong-growing types.

The *alpina, macropetala, montana* and *viticella* cultivars, coupled with the robust-growing, late-flowering species such as *tangutica, tibetana, serratifolia* and *potanini* var. *fargesii* will all tackle the job and succeed. A selection from these clematis will give a good conti-

nuity of flowers throughout the season. One point to remember – if the fence is only one metre high, a *montana* or *tangutica* is suitable but can each cover such a fence to the length of at least eight to nine metres after about three to four years. A selection of *alpina* types and the *viticella* cultivars would be best for a low, one-metre-high fence giving flower from spring until early autumn, with the exception of a few weeks during early summer. The use of a *montana* cultivar on a low wall, possibly alongside a set of garden steps, in association with a variegated-leafed ivy (*Hedera*) will make a colourful addition to any garden.

Growing Clematis in North America

My approach to this chapter is more about climatic conditions than cultural details as these are generally covered in other chapters within the book.

However, travelling in North America on business, to attend Flower Shows and to present lectures during the last 10 years, I have been able to pick up tips from the successful growers of clematis in various locations. I have also learned about the selection of appropriate species and cultivars for the very different climatic conditions.

In Ernest Markham's book entitled 'Clematis' published in 1935, there is a very good chapter written by J. E. Spingarn, who was described by Ernest Markham as "the well-known writer and grower of these climbers on the other side of the Atlantic." Mr Spingarn makes, I believe, a very valuable statement: "The conditions that surround gardening in England are so different from those in the United States and Canada, in climate and soil, in plant diseases and insect pests, and in many other ways, that English garden books are seldom of much practical use to the American gardener. It is this reason that Mr Markham has asked me to contribute a brief chapter on clematis in America: every English garden book should have an American appendix of some sort if it is intended to be read by American as well as English gardeners."

Having read the Spingarn chapter with interest I discovered that in many respects the attitude to growing clematis in these two countries had changed very little until very recently. Certainly the selection of species and cultivars offered today with a few exceptions are still limited to the few tried and tested from 60 or so years ago. However, in the last seven or eight years some leading nurserymen and mail order companies have extended their list of clematis offered for sale.

I have been able to exchange clematis with North American nurserymen and gardeners and recently I have been able to send clematis collections to various botanical gardens in both the United States and Canada for evaluation purposes. Obviously a few more years, a dry summer and a few more very cold winters are needed for these trials to provide helpful information. The trials undertaken at the Chicago Botanical Garden in Illinois have already been most informative.

Historically only certain varieties have been grown in certain areas or

Clematis viticella 'Betty Corning' is a recent introduction from North America.

Clematis 'Gillian Blades' successfully adorns this mailbox.

– that Americans had been slow to use their own native species in their gardens has been confirmed by my own findings and those of Mr John Elsley from South Carolina, who is respected throughout North America as one of their leading plantsmen. Mr Spingarn points out that there are a dozen native species that are worthy of a place in gardens. He noted that *Clematis texensis*, a native of Texas, has been found to be hardy in New York and New England and that it has flowered in Bar Habour and in Ottawa. Sadly 'true' or good forms of this species are not readily available either in Europe or North America. However one of its cultivars *texensis* 'Duchess of Albany' a great favourite of mine proved to be winter hardy in Ontario during the winter of 1993/94 when it recovered and grew after temperatures of –35°C (–30°F). C. *crispa* was also noted by Mr Spingarn as being 'hardy almost anywhere'. This charming species which is a native of the southern states varies in colour a little from pale blue to white and has recurving tips to its tepals. One of the more recent clematis introduced in north America is *viti-cella* 'Betty Corning' which is believed to be a cross between *crispa* and *viticella*. C. *viticella*, a European species introduced into north America in the early part of the nineteenth century, has proved to be winter hardy, to at least –35°C (–30°F), ninety miles north of New York. Therefore it is hoped that *viticella* 'Betty Corning' will have retained the hardiness of its two parents. It has certainly proved successful in Southern Carolina, in the heat and humidity, where I saw it producing its second crop of flowers in early June 1995.

Other North American species that Mr Spingarn noted that I know are generally available and natives of the east are: *pitcheri, reticulata, versicolor, viorna* and the vigorous *ligusticifolia;* and from the western

states as these have been the only ones available. Consequently have wrongly been thought to be the only clematis that would 'survive' or 'do well' in these areas and the lack of evaluation trials have not dispelled this theory.

Mr Spingarn's records and knowledge and that which I have gained in recent years seem to vary very little

and he quotes a list of these varieties that will 'do well' or 'survive' given the extreme heat and cold. I feel it is worth my repeating some of his helpful comments as I believe them to be firm guidelines of what species and cultivars can or are already established in these harsh climates. His conclusion that he drew over sixty years ago

states *columbiana*.

Other species which were introduced into North America before 1935 such as *heracleifolia* var. *davidiana*, *potanini* var. *fargesii*, *integrifolia* var. *integrifolia*, × *jouiniana*, *orientalis*, *serratifolia*, *tangutica* var. *tangutica*, *terniflora*, *vitalba* and *viticella* have all proved to be winter hardy to –35°C (–30°F) ninety miles north of New York.

Mr Spingarn also points out that Dr F Skinner from Dropmore, Manitoba – where temperatures drop to –40°C (–40°F) and occasionally to –51°C (–60°F) had been successful in flowering the following more readily available species: *aethusifolia*, *alpina* var. *alpina*, *alpina* var. *sibirica*, *brevicaudata*, *douglasii* var. *scottii* (now known as *hirsutissima* var. *scottii*), *fusca* var. *fusca*, *ligusticifolia*, *macropetala* var. *macropetala*, *recta* var. *recta*, *serratifolia*, *tangutica* var. *tangutica*, *viorna*, *virginiana*, and *viticella*. Dr Skinner had not been successful in flowering any large flowered cultivars but some of his hybrids of the species had survived. These species included *integrifolia*, *viticella* and *serratifolia*. One of the Skinner cultivars 'Blue Boy', a plant very similar in habit to 'Eriostemon' the first hybrid clematis ever raised in Holland in 1830, is of non-clinging habit and I believe to be the result of a cross between *integrifolia* and *viticella*. Therefore I assume that the cultivar 'Blue Boy' may be winter hardy to –40°C (–40°F). At the time of writing we are flowering dark purple blue, light blue and pale pink seedlings of this cultivar which, if confirmed to be winter hardy, will be valuable garden plants. I have not been as generous as Dr Skinner when I have provided its zone rating in this book; time will tell.

Of course one species, *terniflora* (formerly known as *paniculata* and *maxmowicziana*) has almost naturalized itself in some regions. This species received from Russia in 1877 at the Arnold Arboretum, Massachusetts, is known as the "sweet autumn clematis" and is hardy in zones 5–9.

Therefore with a little trial and error there are a range of species and small-flowered cultivars that can easily be adopted to the cold harsh climate of the northern parts of the United States and cold areas of Canada.

I should now turn my attention to Mr Spingarn's comments about the large-flowered cultivars for the cold north. *Clematis florida* and *florida* 'Sieboldii', introduced into North America before 1840, and forms of *lanuginosa*, introduced soon afterwards, caused interest in clematis but of course the introduction of 'Jackmanii' in Boston in 1866 created an enormous growth of interest in the large-flowered cultivars. Some of the most successful of the older cultivars and those still grown widely today

Clematis **Sugar Candy**™ '*Evione*'®

include: 'Jackmanii', 'Henryi', 'Ramona', 'Madame Edouard André', 'Madame Baron Veillard', 'Gipsy Queen', 'Ville de Lyon' and the double white 'Duchess of Edinburgh'. These all withstood –35°C (–30°F) during the winter of 1933/34, without winter protection. Others which survived with some protection were reported to be 'Belle Nantaise', Fairy Queen', 'Lady Betty Balfour', 'Lady Caroline Neville', 'Mrs Hope', 'Nelly Moser' and the ever popular even today 'Perle d'Azur'. Based on Mr Spingarn's old information which I value highly, and knowledge gained by other growers of these fine clematis cultivars, it is therefore easy to make recommendations for the growing of the above mentioned cultivars as well as clematis of similar habit and flowering periods. However before I deal with this I would like to record a few further cultural conditions that can be borne in mind before species or cultivar selection is made.

With a climate so variable it is difficult to make a general statement that would hold good throughout the United States and Canada. This has proved itself already with other plants such as *Ceanothus* and *Hebe* which are rarely seen grown to perfection on the eastern seaboard. *Clematis montana* and its cultivars are rarely seen performing in North America as well as they do in Europe, in some areas this is obviously due to the winter temperatures and possibly in the south due to high humidity. However, I'm sure that some of the cultivars are successful in many areas. One of the hardiest is *montana* f. *grandiflora* which has been known to flower without snow cover at –29°C (–20°F).

Gardeners in the Pacific North West are fortunate and any clematis that grow successfully in England will grow most successfully here and will be quite winter hardy in Vancouver, Seattle and Portland.

Gardeners in California and other

states with high summer temperatures can grow the tried and tested old cultivars such as 'Ramona', 'Jackmanii' and 'Ville de Lyon' as well as some of the more modern large-flowered cultivars, but naturally Mediterranean species such as *viticella*, *cirrhosa* and *campaniflora* will establish well. Likewise a selection of New Zealand species such as *paniculata*, *forsteri*, × *cartmanii* 'Joe' and some of the Chinese species such as *armandii* are ideal for Southern California and the Gulf States.

Soil is obviously as variable as the climate and ph values should be considered but the thought that clematis will grow only in lime soils should be, I believe, forgotten. Obviously most of the species grow naturally in soils with a moderate to high degree of lime. I believe that because nearly all of the first clematis hybrids grown in gardens were grafted onto either *vitalba* or *viticella* that people wrongly assumed that these cultivars, now grown on their own roots from cuttings, should be treated the same. In woodland soils where azaleas and rhododendrons are growing, clematis can be grown quite happily. If the soil is distinctly acid then a little lime can be added. During the production of

Clematis viticella 'Polish Spirit' provides colourful decoration for this balcony in South Carolina

TIPS FOR GROWING CLEMATIS IN NORTH AMERICAN GARDENS

1. Buy good, strong well grown, well rooted clematis. Short, stocky well-branched plants are best.

2. Plant in the early spring so that plants become fully established by early fall and that way they will survive the hard winters.

3. Check the zone ratings before purchase.

4. Select well drained soils, or improve the soil conditions for better drainage.

5. If you grow the early, large-flowered types be prepared to lose the first flowers some springs but wait for the first crop of flowers from the new growth in early summer, all will not be lost.

6. Cover the stems and root crown with straw or other material until snowfall.

7. Carefully take down the old stems from the summer and cover them with straw until deep snow cover, this may help retain the old growth from a good crop of early summer flowers from the previous season's stems.

8. Do not always expect the clematis to reach the height as given for growing the plants under English conditions.

9. Protect your container-grown clematis over winter to retain the previous season's stems.

10. Always plant the root crown 5–7.5cm (2–3 inches) deeper than the soil level in the containers, this will build up a root crown below soil level for extra winter protection and help to prevent the clematis dying from clematis wilt.

Clematis terniflora is one of the most popular species grown in American gardens.

TIPS FOR GROWING CLEMATIS IN HOT SUNNY CLIMATES

1. Buy good, strong well grown plants. Short, stocky well-branched plants are best.

2. Plant in the fall or very early spring for early establishment.

3. Improve the soil on very dry sandy free draining soils.

4. Select native species or New Zealand and Mediterranean species.

5. Select the early spring *alpina* and *macropetala* types, the early large flowered cultivars that flower before high summer and the *viticella* cultivars that seem to enjoy the warmer climates.

6. Make sure the root crown is well shaded from the sun, be prepared to water freely in spring and early fall.

7. When planting, plant at extra depth as for those clematis for harsher climates.

8. Be prepared to have darker coloured flowers due to heat or humidity.

9. Plant pale coloured clematis out of strong sunshine.

10. Look out for some of the new large-flowered cultivars, that are similar in habit to those already growing in your area.

11. Select other varieties that come under the same sections as those already grown successfully in your garden to give a wider choice.

clematis in containers in our nursery the average ph is 5.5.

Clematis, although requiring plenty of water during the hot spring and summer weather, also succeed better on free draining soils especially during severe winters. The large flowered cultivars, as do the species, always enjoy and perform better when their root systems are shaded. In their natural wild habitat clematis species are found growing out from under rocks, bushes or small trees etc, which give moisture and shade to the root system. This therefore must be borne in mind when planting clematis in very hot climates.

Clematis are ideal plants for growing in containers for the patio, small town garden or deck garden and full cultural details are given on page 78–122. However in North America a few extra cultural instructions are necessary. The species or cultivar

Clematis montana 'Elizabeth' adorning a low wall.

selection can be the same as for Europe, the *alpina*, *macropetala* types for the spring months and the early large-flowered cultivars described in Section 4 on page 91 are the most ideal. Also included are the early large-flowered double and semi-double types in Section 5. Bear in mind that while the pale pinks fade more quickly in sun than the darker colours, they can be used to advantage to give lightness and colour to a shady north-facing area.

The hardy *alpina* and *macropetala* types will be quite winter hardy unless the climate is severe and they can be left outside over winter (ie they will flower well if the lowest winter temperature is about −18°C (0°F), if temperatures are likely to drop lower, then some winter protection is best). The early large-flowered cultivars should be protected if the lowest winter temperatures are likely to drop below about −10°C (−14°F). It is very important to retain as much old growth as possible so that the maximum amount of spring flowers can be produced.

If plants are left outside with no protection the leaf axil buds (produced by fall) will be damaged reducing the amount of spring flowers. A shed or outbuilding with frost protection is required, the building should be well lit if possible and the plants can be moved inside by late fall and before the onset of winter. The plants should be slowly exposed to normal outdoor conditions in early spring before leaf development. Although this involves some work the gardener will be rewarded with an outstanding crop of spring and early summer flowers. Clematis may be a frustrating plant to some gardeners but care, attention to detail, especially watering, is all that is needed. A gardener I know, Jim McNairn in Greenwood, South Carolina started gardening only six years ago, and the success he has obtained by attending to detail is outstanding. He has grown a range of twenty or more clematis of all types through trees, over fences and on his house and his success rate in establishing plants does him credit, I should add he is an ardent reader of my books!

Clematis growing in North America is very much on the increase and success rates for establishment of plants is high. Swap and exchange information with your garden centre owner, the nurseryman, with the mail order companies you buy your plants from and from fellow gardeners. I too shall be more than happy to hear from successful and unsuccessful growers in the interest of the successful cultivation of this marvellous genus.

SUGGESTED CLEMATIS FOR NORTH AMERICAN GARDENS

Within this book there are a great many clematis discussed and described, some of which are not generally available in nurseries and garden centres in North America. I therefore feel it will be helpful to those gardeners trying to find their way through great lists of clematis if I make some recommendations as to the better clematis for North American gardens. The following list of species and cultivars have been kept in their flowering groups for ease of selection.

The Evergreen Species and Cultivars

These can be grown only in mild locations in Zones 7–9, such as south-west British Columbia, Washington, Oregon and California.
armandii
cirrhosa 'Freckles'

The Early-flowering Species and their Cultivars

The *alpina* and *macropetala* types are some of the most reliable and winter hardy clematis for all areas.
alpina 'Constance'
alpina 'Frankie'
alpina 'Helsingborg'
alpina 'Pink Flamingo'
alpina 'Willy'
macropetala var. *macropetala*
macropetala 'Pauline'
macropetala 'Lagoon'
macropetala 'Markham's Pink'
macropetala 'White Wings'

The *montanas* have not generally established well in North America, except in favourable growing conditions within Zones 7–9.
montana 'Elizabeth'
montana 'Freda'
montana f. *grandiflora*
montana 'Tetrarose'
montana var. *rubens*
montana var. *rubens* 'Odorata'

The Early, Double, Semi-double and Mid-season Large-flowered Clematis

This large group of clematis produces their main crop of flowers from the previous season's ripened stems. However, after severe winters the previous season's stems may be killed to ground level. If this occurs, the clematis will flower later in the season on the current season's stems, producing smaller flowers but in the same profusion. They are hardy in Zones 4–9.

Clematis grown in containers in cold climates will need the protection of a shed or outbuilding to give frost protection, so the previous season's ripened stems are not damaged or killed by frost or dessicated by freezing winds.

Early Large-flowered Cultivars
Anna Louise™ 'Evithree'®*
'Bees' Jubilee'*
'Carnaby'*
'Dr Ruppel'*
'Elsa Späth'*
'Fireworks'*
'Gillian Blades'*
'H. F. Young'*
'Lasturstern'*
'Masquerade'*
'Miss Bateman'*
'Nelly Moser'*
'Niobe'*
Royal Velvet™ 'Evifour'®*
Sugar Candy™ 'Evione'®
'Sunset'*
'The President'*
'Will Goodwin'*

Double and Semi-double Large-flowered Cultivars
Arctic Queen™ 'Evitwo'®*†
'Daniel Deronda'*
'Duchess of Edinburgh'†
'Mrs George Jackman'*
'Multiblue'*†
'Royalty'*

Mid-season Large-flowered Cultivars
'General Sikorski'
'Henryi'
'Marie Boisselot'
'Ramona'
'Violet Charm'

The Late Large-flowered Cultivars

This group is very useful and versatile, and a little more winter hardy than the early large-flowered cultivars. Zones 3–9.
'Ascotiensis'*
'Comtesse de Bouchaud'
'Ernest Markham'
'Gipsy Queen'
'Hagley Hybrid'*
'Jackmanii'
'John Huxtable'
'Perle d'Azure'
'Perrin's Pride'*
'Pink Fantasy'*
'Prince Charles'*
'Victoria'
'Voluceau'

The Clematis Viticella Group

An extremely valuable group for North American gardens. They do not suffer from clematis wilt and can be used in many different garden locations.
viticella 'Abundance'
viticella 'Alba Luxurians'
viticella 'Betty Corning'*
viticella 'Etoile Violette'
viticella 'Madame Julia Correvon'*
viticella 'Polish Spirit'
viticella 'Purpurea Plena Elegans'
viticella 'Royal Velours'
viticella 'Venosa Violacea'*

---

* indicates also suitable for container culture

† produce double flowers on new growth

The Late-flowering Species and their Small-flowered Cultivars

Clematis in this section are very diverse in their habit, leaf, flower form, and height, and have differing garden uses. Their full descriptions, on pages 81-122 should be consulted before final selection.

'Blue Boy'
crispa
'Durandii'
'Eriostemon'
'Paul Farges' Summer Snow
integrifolia var. *integrifolia*
integrifolia 'Rosea'
× *jouiniana* 'Praecox'
Petit Faucon™ 'Evisix'®
recta var. *recta*
tangutica 'Bill Mackenzie'
terniflora
texensis 'Duchess of Albany'
texensis 'Gravetye Beauty'
× *triternata* 'Rubromarginata'
viorna

Clematis 'Marie Boisselot' provides a perfect foil for this mailbox.

The following list is of the clematis which have performed best in the trials held in the Chicago Botanical Gardens.

alpina 'Pamela Jackman'
'Ascotiensis'
'Barbara Jackman'
'Bees' Jubilee'**
tangutica 'Bill Mackenzie'
'Comtesse de Bouchaud'**
'Countess of Lovelace'
'Durandii'**
'Elsa Späth'

'Ernest Markham'
'Gypsy Queen'
'Guernsey Cream'
'Hagley Hybrid'
× *jouiniana* 'Praecox'**
'Lady Betty Balfour'
macropetala var. *macropetala***
'Marie Boisselot'
'Madame Baron Veillard'
'Mrs Cholmondeley'
'Mrs P. B. Truax'
'Nelly Moser'
'Pagoda'
'Perle d'Azure'

recta var. *recta*
'Rouge Cardinal'
serratifolia
'The President'
tibetana var. *tibetana*
'Ville de Lyon'**
viticella 'Etoile Violette'**
viticella 'Södertälje' (syn. *v.* 'Grandiflora Sanguinea')**
'Vyvyan Pennell'**

**Superior performance

Clematis
as a
Cut Flower

Surprisingly clematis are not often used in flower arrangements but the strikingly beautiful flowers are complemented by elegant foliage and interesting seed-heads, both of which, like the flowers, can be used in many types of arrangements.

The colour range extends from pure white to deepest purple, through all the shades of blue, pink and mauve plus the creams, lemon-yellow and greens. Apart from this bounty of colour there are many forms to choose from, for instance there are both double and single large-flowered forms, the *alpinas* and some *texensis* with nodding heads, the four-tepalled *montanas* and the herbaceous clematis like the easy to condition and use *heracleifolia* var. *davidiana* with its strong stems and clusters of clear blue flowers. One more possibility is the sweetly scented *flammula* with its long strands of tiny white flowers.

Clematis can be found flowering throughout the year but, for use as a cut flower, most arrangers will rely on the outdoor season which starts in spring with the *alpinas* and finishes in mid autumn with the *tangutical tibetana* cultivars.

The foliage of *Clematis armandii*, an evergreen clematis from China, is most handsome. The large, linear-shaped dark green leaflets have a most unusual, strong, leathery texture. If stems of one metre are picked they are useful for pedestal arrangements when the arranger is in need of a strand of something to hang downwards. The evergreen foliage of *cirrhosa* var. *cirrhosa* and *cirrhosa* var. *balearica* can be also used for this same purpose. The fern-leafed clematis, as this Mediterranean species is sometimes called, is most delicate, especially the very fine cut-leafed form *cirrhosa* var. *balearica*. The shorter pieces of this and many other types of clematis can be used in smaller arrangements. Clematis foliage and seed-heads are especially effective in table arrangements where their form and their subtle colour can be appreciated.

When selecting a clematis flower from the garden for picking, one should choose a flower which has a thick, strong stem, not one which will

This arrangement of clematis species and small-flowered hybrids would grace any room.

bend when picked; otherwise, due to the structure of a weak stem, the flower may collapse within hours of picking. Choose a flower that has just opened or, if possible, one that is three-quarters of the way open at the point when the tepals are about to expand to their full size. When an open flower is picked, beware of the condition of the centre of the flower: the stamens should still be held together and not have started to unfold toward the base of the tepals.

After selecting the perfect young flower and the stem has been cut from the plant – the length is not important – the foliage should be removed to reduce transpiration from the leaves. The stem should be placed immediately into cold water, as deeply as possible, and the flowers can then be conditioned in this cold water, if possible overnight. Depending upon the situation of the flower arrangement and the room condition, clematis flowers that I have used have been known to last for ten days; however, four to five days is the average time.

In the past, I have used clematis as cut flowers in exhibits at the Chelsea Flower Show. The flowers were conditioned well before they were transported and arranged, and some have lasted the full five days of the show – which is indeed remarkable given the heat and conditions of an exhibit under canvas!

While using cut flowers in this way, I have grown plants specially in beds in a cold glasshouse, using a little heat to bring the flowers on and to open at the correct time. If the reader is fortunate enough to have the space available in a conservatory or cold glasshouse, growing clematis in this way for cut flowers is most rewarding. When clematis are grown in soil beds under glasshouse conditions, periods

THE MOST SUCCESSFUL CLEMATIS FOR CUT FLOWERS

Early Large-flowered Cultivars
Anna Louise™ 'Evithree'®
'Barbara Jackman'
Blue Moon™ 'Evirin'®
'Dawn'
'Dr Ruppel'
'Edith'
'Elsa Späth'
Evening Star™ 'Evista'®
'Fireworks'
'Gillian Blades'
'Guernsey Cream'
'Haku Ookan'
'Horn of Plenty'
'Kathleen Wheeler'
'Ken Donson'
'Lasurstern'
'Masquerade'
'Miss Bateman'
'Mrs Cholmondeley'
'Nelly Moser'
'Niobe'
'Richard Pennell'
Royal Velvet™ 'Evifour'®
'Ruby Glow'
'Scartho Gem'
'Snow Queen'
Sugar Candy™ 'Evione'®
'The President'
Vino™ 'Poulvo'®
'Will Goodwin'

Doubles & Semi-Double Large-flowered Cultivars
Arctic Queen™ 'Evitwo'®
'Belle of Woking'
'Duchess of Edinburgh'
Josephine™ 'Evijohill'®
'Kiri Te Kanawa
'Lady Caroline Nevill'
'Louise Rowe'
'Multiblue'
'Veronica's Choice'
'Vyvyan Pennell'

Mid-season Large-flowered Cultivars
'Belle Nantaise'
'General Sikorski'
'Henryi'
'Marie Boisselot'
'Prins Hendrik'
'Violet Charm'
'W. E. Gladstone'

Late Large-flowered Cultivars
'Pink Fantasy'
'Prince Charles'

Viticella Cultivars
viticella 'Alba Luxurians'
viticella 'Blue Belle'
viticella 'Madame Julia Correvon'
viticella 'Minuet'
viticella 'Polish Spirit'
viticella 'Purpurea Plena Elegans'
viticella 'Royal Velours'
viticella 'Venosa Violacea'

Late-flowering Species and their Cultivars
'Durandii'
flammula
florida Pistachio™ 'Evirida'®
florida 'Plena'
florida 'Sieboldii'
heracleifolia 'Cote d'Azure'
heracleifolia var. davidiana
heracleifolia var. d. 'Wyevale'
'Huldine'
Petit Faucon™ 'Evisix'®
tangutica var. tangutica
tangutica 'Bill Mackenzie'
terniflora
texensis 'Duchess of Albany'
texensis 'Etoile Rose'
texensis 'Gravetye Beauty'
texensis 'Sir Trevor Lawrence'

of long high temperatures should be avoided; the best clematis for picking are those which have been grown under almost outdoor conditions, but with protection from wind and rain. Clematis grown in this way will be several weeks ahead of outdoor plants. Hard pruning of all clematis grown specially for cut flowers is important, as strong new growth needs to be encouraged; and even established, early large-flowered cultivars should be pruned down to about one metre in early spring.

After many of the clematis flowers have died away they are often replaced by delightful fluffy seed heads. If the old flower head and flower stalks remain and are not trimmed off, within several weeks the pollinated seeds begin to grow. As the seed tails mature and become a silvery-grey colour, they add yet another attractive dimension to the clematis plant. As the seed heads become of interest to the flower arranger, they may be cut for immediate use or preserved for dried winter arrangements.

If you are particularly interested in growing clematis with attractive seed heads, then the early-flowering types are some of the best. The semi-hardy *napaulensis*, which flowers in December, has delightful large seed heads in mid winter and late winter when grown under cold glasshouse conditions in England. Both the *alpina* and *macropetala* types have seed heads from late spring onwards and these look charming. As the occasional summer flowers are produced by these clematis, so one has a mix of flowers and seed heads. Most of the early large-flowered cultivars, such as 'Nelly Moser', 'Ken Donson', and 'Daniel Deronda' have more rounded seed heads from mid summer onwards.

Clematis 'Fireworks', a strong-growing early large-flowered cultivar.

The striking seed heads of Clematis 'Ken Donson'

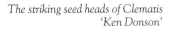

The later-flowering, large-flowered types, sadly do not have such attractive seed heads. So, from the large-flowered types, one must choose plants that flower before mid summer to be sure of getting this added bonus. The later-flowering species, such as *tangutica* var. *tangutica* all of the *tibetana* cultivars, *serratifolia* and, of course, the European native *vitalba*, are among some of the best, as are *virginiana* and *terniflora* in the U.S.A. The latter is absolutely gorgeous when in full seed.

Both *virginiana* and *vitalba* have many common names; one of the best, I think, is "old man's beard" which really describes the mass of seed heads that this plant has during the late autumn months. To see a *vitalba* covered with seed heads, clambering over a hedgerow in England in December covered in frost on a bright morning, is a great delight.

Preserving seed heads

The most reliable clematis for this purpose are the early-flowering species and early large-flowered cultivars whose seed-heads are fully developed but have not gone fluffy by late summer. Later-flowering species and cultivars are more at risk from the damp conditions which usually prevail as the season advances.

Stems can be cut when the seed-heads are in the silky stage and preserved by drying or by using glycerine. Stems with seed heads attached can be dried by hanging them upside down in a dry atmosphere. This may take several weeks. To glycerine them, put the freshly cut stem ends in a mixture of one third glycerine and two-thirds boiling water. Stir to mix thoroughly and use while it is still very hot. The mixture should be about 5cm deep in a jam jar or similar container. The stalks and any leaves will turn a rich brown colour while the seedheads will be slightly paler and keep their silky texture. Imperfect foliage should be removed and stems should not be packed too tightly.

The jar needs to be placed in a cool but dry place, out of bright light and a check should be made on progress every few days, the mixture being topped up if necessary.

The stems are ready when the colour is even and the leaves are just slightly oily to the touch. Do not put these or dried stems in water or a damp atmosphere. Long trails of *vitalba* seedheads can be treated in this way but all seedheads must be cut before they reach the fluffy stage.

SOME OF THE MOST NOTEWORTHY CLEMATIS FOR PRODUCING ATTRACTIVE SEED HEADS

Early-flowering Species and their Cultivars
alpina 'Columbine'
alpina 'Constance'
alpina 'Foxy'
alpina 'Frankie'
alpina 'Pink Flamingo'
alpina 'White Columbine'
macropetala var. *macropetala*
macropetala 'Markham's Pink'
macropetala 'White Moth'

Early Large-flowered Cultivars
'Bees' Jubilee'
Blue Moon™ 'Evirin'®
'Corona'
'Dawn'
'Dr Ruppel'
'Edith'
'Edouard Desfossé'
'Etoile de Paris'

'Gillian Blades'
'Haku Ookan'
'H. F. Young'
'Horn of Plenty'
'Kathleen Wheeler'
'Ken Donson'
'Lasurstern'
'Marcel Moser'
'Masquerade'
'Miss Bateman'
'Moonlight'
'Mrs Cholmondeley'
'Mrs P. B. Truax'
'Nelly Moser'
'Pink Champagne'
'The President'
'Wada's Primrose'

Doubles & Semi-Double Large-flowered Cultivars
Arctic Queen™ 'Evitwo'®
'Daniel Deronda'
'Mrs George Jackman'
'Vyvyan Pennell'

Late-flowering Species and their Cultivars
flammula
Golden Tiara® 'Kugotia'
heracleifolia 'Cote d'Azure'
integrifolia var. *integrifolia*
Petit Faucon™ 'Evisix'®
recta var. *recta*
recta var. *purpurea*
rehderiana
tangutica var. *tangutica*
tangutica 'Bill Mackenzie'
tangutica 'Helios'
terniflora
vitalba

Propagation

The propagation of clematis is a challenging and satisfying occupation for the keen clematis grower.

There are several ways in which clematis may be reproduced: by seed, layering, cuttings, grafting and by root crown division of the herbaceous cultivars.

Reproduction by layering

The layering of clematis is not as exciting as waiting for seedlings to flower but it is a means by which a gardener can successfully, and without much experience, increase the numbers of clematis for his own garden, or to use for swopping with other gardeners. The exchange of plants between gardening enthusiasts is always a satisfactory means of increasing one's own selection and is a way in which plants gain wider distribution.

The best time for layering clematis is during late spring or very early summer. A 15cm diameter flowerpot should be sunk into the soil near to the base of the clematis plant and within easy reach of the stem which is to be layered. The pot should contain a mixture of John Innes potting soil No. 2, filled to the top and lightly firmed. The selected stem should be gently bent downwards towards the pot, and the nearest node to the flowerpot should then be pinned into the soil with a piece of thick wire. Before the node is pinned down it should be split using a sharp knife – a 2.5cm cut made in an upward direction from below the node and into the node will help rooting to take place. If the cut and stem surrounding it are dusted with a rooting hormone, this will assist in faster rooting. When the stem is pinned onto the soil in the pot, an extra layer of soil can be placed over the node and a stone may also be placed over the wire pin to hold it in place.

Rooting of the stem may take several weeks and the soil in the flowerpot must not be allowed to become dry. After about nine months the layered stem will have formed a new plant; but it should be left attached to its parent until early

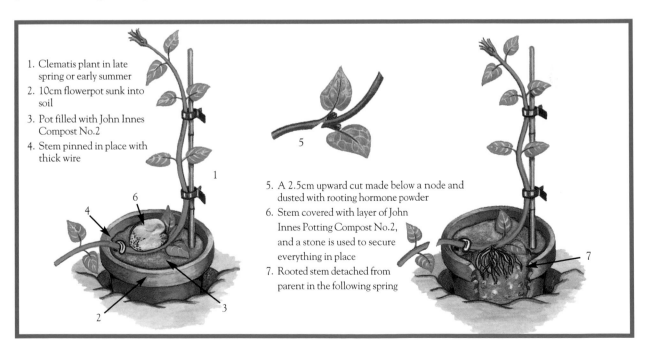

1. Clematis plant in late spring or early summer
2. 10cm flowerpot sunk into soil
3. Pot filled with John Innes Compost No.2
4. Stem pinned in place with thick wire
5. A 2.5cm upward cut made below a node and dusted with rooting hormone powder
6. Stem covered with layer of John Innes Potting Compost No.2, and a stone is used to secure everything in place
7. Rooted stem detached from parent in the following spring

Layering

Clematis seed sown in pots, each covered with a fine layer of grit.

spring, when it may be detached and the pot removed from the soil. The new plant should then be planted as if it were a plant purchased from a nursery and pruned as described on pages 22 to 27.

Reproduction by seed

All clematis species may be grown successfully from seed. The resultant seedlings are generally true to type, but there may be variation, either improvements or poorer forms of the plant from which the seed was collected. Obviously no clematis cultivars can be reproduced true to type from seed because they are hybrids. However, this does not deter the enthusiastic gardener who uses this disadvantage in the hope of raising a brand new clematis cultivar.

Seedlings from clematis cultivars are certainly exciting because one does not know what to expect with regard to the possible colours. Seeds collected from a blue clematis may produce white, or even pink flowers.

One is, therefore, left in expectation until the flower of the seedling opens, resulting in either success or disappointment. In fact, a cultivar now generally available called 'Edith', a large-white clematis with red anthers, was raised by me and was just a chance seedling from 'Mrs Cholmondeley', a pale blue cultivar.

Seed can be collected from the early-flowering clematis in early autumn as soon as it becomes swollen, brown and ripened. The gardener can judge when the seeds are ripened by the condition of the seed tails. As the seeds ripen these seed tails become fluffy and are silky-grey in colour. The swollen seeds vary in size depending upon the cultivar and they are mostly dark brown in colour, breaking away from the old flower stalk when fully ripened.

Seeds of the later-flowering species and cultivars do not have the opportunity to become fully ripened by early autumn unless the weather is hot and sunny; therefore, the early-flowering

types are the ones to experiment with first.

Seed collected during early to mid autumn may be sown in seed trays or pots immediately after collecting and removing the seed tails. Seed compost to the John Innes seed compost formula may be used and the seeds need to be covered by compost to a depth of 5mm. The container should be placed in a cold frame or glasshouse until germination takes place, which may take up to 12 months with some cultivars. During this time the top of the container should be covered with a piece of glass and brown paper and the compost must not be allowed to dry out.

As soon as germination takes place the seedlings must be given more sunlight, and as soon as they become large enough to transplant they should be potted into a 7.5cm flowerpot and grown on in a similar manner to tomatoes or other seedlings. Twelve months after germination they may be planted out into a

Removing unnecessary foliage.

Cuttings ready for inserting.

garden position or grown on in a larger flowerpot (John Innes No. 2 potting compost) until they flower. It may take up to four years from collection of seed until the first mature flowers are produced. The waiting and patience is not always rewarded by a brand new cultivar worthy of commercial production and sales but, I assure you, the excitement from when the first flower bud appears until the flower opens is almost too much to bear.

Reproduction by root division

This is a simple means of increasing the herbaceous clematis and may be done as soon as the soil is frost free in the very early spring before bud break. An established plant may be dug up from its position and, by the use of two forks placed back to back the clematis can be divided. Each piece of plant detached from the original should have roots and an old stem on which new growth buds are visible. The divided plants can then be replanted immediately and given similar treatment to a new clematis planted out from a container. It is vital to keep the divided plant's small root system moist until it becomes established.

Reproduction by cuttings

This method of propagation is for the experienced gardener and the professional nurseryman. An internodal cutting is used with the cutting taken from the soft, young stems during late spring or early summer, from plants growing in an open garden position. Propagation from cuttings of the vigorous species is reasonably easy. However the large-flowered cultivars are rather more difficult. For success-ful rooting of cuttings a warm humid position, out of direct sunlight, is necessary.

Reproduction by grafting

Clematis reproduction by the use of grafting is now outdated and used only by some nurserymen, when cultivars are difficult to root from cuttings. Clematis *vitalba* ("old man's beard") and *viticella* are the usual root stocks used by professional growers when grafting is practised. If grafted plants are damaged by mice or affected by "clematis wilt", they have little chance of full recovery and this is the reason why this means of reproduction has been more or less phased out.

Pests and Diseases

Fortunately, clematis plants are less prone to disease or attacks by pests than many other plants, for which the clematis grower can be thankful. Like other shrubs and semi-woody plants, clematis are subject to attacks from aphid, mildew and other small pests, all of which can be easily controlled by using traditional methods without causing harm to the clematis plant.

Greenfly attacks can be easily controlled.

Clematis Wilt

The only major problem and sometimes cause of distress to the clematis and gardener is clematis wilt. The wilt is caused by a fungus, *Phoma clematidina*, entering a damaged part of the stem. What previously has appeared to be a healthy plant suddenly collapses. Sometimes only a small part of a plant is affected but in some extreme cases the entire plant suffers. Unfortunately, little research has been carried out to find a cure and only preventative action can be taken. However, with much healthier plants being available in garden centres and nurseries, this is becoming less of a problem in gardens.

The point at which "wilt" affects the plant is generally near soil level or at least within one metre of soil level. The fungus is thought to be present in the soil previous to the attack and possibly splashed into a damaged stem which may have been twisted or cracked by wind or during cultivation. Once the fungus is positioned in its host, it grows, blocking the sap stream and causing the stem above to collapse due to lack of moisture.

If such damage should occur, all affected stems and foliage must be removed immediately and burnt. Afterwards, any remaining stems can be sprayed with Bio Supercarb as a possible preventative measure against further damage. The foliage and lower stems of the plant and surrounding soil area may be treated every four weeks until the plant has recovered and produced new growth, or no further collapse by "clematis wilt" is experienced.

If a plant consistently "wilts" then it is best dug up, the soil removed from the root system and the plant submerged in a Bio Supercarb (carbendazim) solution. The treated plant can be carefully replanted in another site, and the original site should be treated again with Bio Supercarb, as a precaution against further attacks on plants replanted in the same postion. If "clematis wilt" has become a problem in a particular garden, the preventative measures described can be used to reduce the risk of future damage.

Generally only unhealthy, old or young weak plants are affected, and in most cases the clematis recovers fully within two years. New growth is produced from above or just below soil level. The important point made earlier regarding the extra depth of planting, allowing several nodes to be placed under the soil level, was intended to help the plant when damage occurs near ground level. With the extra depth of planting, new growth from the dormant buds which remain below soil level can almost be guaranteed, even after all top growth has been removed. Correct and hard pruning of clematis in the earlier years of the plant's life also helps to prevent "wilt" from being fatal and assists with a quick recovery. As new growth appears and produces 2–3 nodes, the tip growth should be pinched out. This will encourage extra stems to be produced. The plant will become more bushy and the growth will become woody and less likely to succumb to further attacks.

Slugs and snails

These delightful little beasts can be very troublesome during early spring, eating pieces out of leaves and skimming stems of young fleshy plants. The asparagus-like shoots produced by the late-flowering species and cultivars are exactly what the slugs have been waiting patiently for all winter, so be warned! There are many slug baits and pellets available but a far cheaper preventative measure is to place a circle of spent coal ashes on the soil near to the main stems of the clematis, keeping the ashes at least 8–10cm from the stems. The coarseness of the ashes is unpleasant to the underparts of a slug or snail, and prevents them from crossing to where the young stems are growing.

Mice and rabbits

These slightly larger creatures also enjoy a supper or breakfast of clematis shoots and the mice also appear to like clematis stems for nesting material. Their control is therefore vital, though not always easy. To prevent rabbits, a collar of very fine mesh netting placed around the stem to a height of one metre usually does the trick. When mice are a big problem, a land drain placed over the clematis root systems allows the top growth to grow through the upturned pipe and will deter mice from constant attack. When the clematis stems have become strong and woody after two years or so, the pipe, if it is unsightly, may be broken and removed because the woody stems are not so attractive to mice.

Earwigs

The plants most prone to earwig damage are those growing through a densely-foliaged evergreen, or on an old wall or outbuilding, where there are plenty of places for the earwigs to hide during daylight. The proprietary products available for their control can be used if damage is extensive. The damage is identified by holes in the foliage or a hole in the unopened flower bud. When a flower bud is the target, a hole is drilled through into a cavity and in some cases the stamens are removed at differing lengths.

Brown/dead leaves on the lower stems

Frequently gardeners become concerned by mid to late summer, or before if the season is dry with little rain, by the lower leaves drying and dying off.

This is not a disease problem but purely a sign that the plant has experienced very dry soil conditions. The cause is therefore one of lack of water and nothing else. Clematis require 9 litres (2 gallons) every other day in drought conditions in free-draining soils, especially at the base of a south-facing wall. Newly planted clematis require regular watering until they become established, especially under trees where the rain does not penetrate.

Here are two examples of powdery mildew, the photograph on the right showing a more advanced stage.

Glossary

Listed below are 339 of the most popular and interesting clematis species and their cultivars, and these have been grouped into nine sections according to their type.

The first table is a quick alphabetical guide which shows at a glance which of the nine sections the 339 different clematis belong to.

Then each of the clematis from the nine sections are elaborated on. First you will find a brief introduction about the general habit of the plants in that section, information about pruning and more detail about the individual flower and its cultivation. The flowering times are referred to in seasons rather than months. The table below shows the relationship of season to month. The flowering times are those in England.

Hardiness Zones

The hardiness zones recommended are based on experience gained by my gardener friends in the USA and Canada. These must be treated as a guideline only, as much more experience is required with the many species and cultivars that are relatively new to cultivation in these areas. Plant hardiness zones are of relevance to countries which have a wide variation in climate, particularly to the USA. These zones have been specified by the United States Department of Agriculture and are based on the average minimum temperature for each zone. Canadian hardiness zones are 'plus one' zone compared with USA zones, eg. 4 becomes 5. The table below gives the zone rating and their equivalent temperature range. These zones indicate the areas where it is expected that the plant will perform

consistently. However, it is important to remember that many climatic factors can effect the tolerance of the plants to the site and these zones can give only a rough guide. Common sense should be used when positioning your plant bearing in mind that, for example an exposed site within one zone will actually reduce the tolerance level to a lower zone than the recommended one.

♛ Award of Garden Merit

The clematis species or cultivars which have been awarded The Royal Horticultural Society's Award of Garden Merit have been denoted with the above symbol. This award is given when the plants have fulfilled all the following criteria as well as having undergone a period of assessment:

* It should be excellent for ordinary garden use (either in the open or under glass).
* It should be of good constitution.
* It should be available in the horticultural trade, or be available for propagation.
* It should not be particularly susceptible to any pest or disease.
* It should not require specialised care other than the provision of appropriate growing conditions for the type of plant concerned (eg. lime-free soil when required).
* It should not be subject to an unreasonable degree of reversion in its vegetative or floral characteristics.

January	February	March	April	May	June
Winter	Late winter	Early spring	Spring	Late spring	Early summer
July	August	September	October	November	December
Summer	Late summer	Early autumn	Autumn	Late autumn	Early winter

RANGE OF AVERAGE ANNUAL MINIMUM TEMPERATURE FOR EACH ZONE

Zone 2	−50°F to −40°F	−45°C to −40°C
Zone 3	−40°F to −30°F	−40°C to −35°C
Zone 4	−30°F to −20°F	−35°C to −29°C
Zone 5	−20°F to −10°F	−29°C to −23°C
Zone 6	−10°F to 0°F	−23°C to −18°C
Zone 7	0°F to 10°F	−18°C to −12°C
Zone 8	10°F to 20°F	−12°C to −7°C
Zone 9	20°F to 30°F	−7°C to −1°C
Zone 10	30°F to 40°F	−1°C to 4°C
Zone 11	Above 40°F	Above 4°C

("s" refers to zones where southern regions only are suitable.)

BCS
C of M
1998
British Clematis Society
Certificate of Merit (date varies)

THE A-Z LIST OF SPECIES AND CULTIVARS

Key to Sections

Section 1	Evergreen and Early Flowering Species	p81	} Pruning Group 1
Section 2	Alpina and Macropetala Types	p84	
Section 3	Montana Types	p88	
Section 4	Early Large-Flowered Cultivars	p91	} Pruning Group 2
Section 5	Double and Semi-double Cultivars	p101	
Section 6	Mid-Season Large-Flowered Cultivars	p105	
Section 7	Later Flowering Large-Flowered	p109	} Pruning Group 3
Section 8	Viticella Types	p113	
Section 9	Late-Flowered Species and Their Forms	p116	

Variety	Section
addisonii	9
aesthusifolia	9
afoliata	1
akebioides	9
Alabast™ 'Poulala'®	4
'Alionushka'	9
'Allanah'	7
alpina var. *alpina*	2
alpina 'Albiflora'	2
alpina 'Blue Dancer'	2
alpina 'Burford White'	2
alpina 'Columbine'	2
alpina 'Constance'	2
alpina 'Cyanea'	2
alpina 'Foxy'	2
alpina 'Frankie'	2
alpina 'Helsingborg'	2
alpina 'Jacqueline du Pré'	2
alpina 'Pamela Jackman'	2
alpina 'Pink Flamingo'	2
alpina 'Ruby'	2
alpina 'Tage Lundell'	2
alpina 'White Columbine'	2
alpina 'Willy'	2
alpina var. *ochotensis*	2
alpina var. *o.* 'Carmen Rose'	2
alpina var. *o.* 'Frances Rivis'	2
alpina var. *sibirica*	2
'Anna'	4
Anna Louise™ 'Evithree'®	4
'Arabella'	9
Arctic Queen™ 'Evitwo'®	5
armandii	1
armandii 'Apple Blossom'	1
armandii 'Jefferies'	1
× *aromatica*	9
'Asao'	4
'Ascotiensis'	7
australis	1
'Barbara Dibley'	4
'Barbara Jackman'	4
'Beauty of Richmond'	6
'Beauty of Worcester'	5
'Bees' Jubilee'	4
'Belle Nantaise'	6
'Belle of Woking'	5

Variety	Section
'Blue Angel'	7
'Blue Boy'	9
Blue Moon™ 'Evirin'®	4
'Blue Ravine'	6
brachiata	9
brevicaudata	9
'Burma Star'	4
campaniflora	8
campaniflora 'Lisboa'	8
'Cardinal Wyszynski'	7
'Carnaby'	4
'Caroline'	4
× *cartmanii* **Avalanche**™ 'Blaaval'®	1
× *cartmanii* 'Joe'	1
'Charissima'	4
chiisanensis	2
chrysocoma var. *chrysocoma*	3
chrysocoma 'Continuity'	3
chrysocoma hybrid	3
cirrhosa var. *cirrhosa*	1
cirrhosa 'Freckles'	1
cirrhosa 'Ourika Valley'	1
cirrhosa 'Wisley Cream'	1
cirrhosa var. *balearica*	1
columbiana var. *tenuiloba*	2
'Comtesse de Bouchaud'	7
connata	9
'Corona'	4
'Countess of Lovelace'	5
'Crimson King'	6
crispa	9
'Daniel Deronda'	5
'Dawn'	4
'Dorothy Tolver'	4
'Dorothy Walton'	7
'Dr. Ruppel'	4
'Duchess of Edinburgh'	5
'Duchess of Sutherland'	6
'Durandii'	9
'Edith'	4
'Edomurasaki'	6
'Edouard Desfossé'	4
'Elgar'	4
'Elsa Späth'	4
'Empress of India'	6
'Eriostemon'	9

Variety	Section
'Ernest Markham'	7
'Etoile de Malicorne'	6
'Etoile de Paris'	4
Evening Star™ 'Evista'®	4
'Fair Rosamond'	4
'Fairy Queen'	6
finetiana	1
'Fireworks'	4
flammula	9
florida **Pistachio**™ 'Evirida'®	9
florida 'Plena'	9
florida 'Sieboldii'	9
forsteri	1
fruticosa	9
'Fujimusume'	4
fusca var. *fusca*	9
fusca var. *violacea*	9
'General Sikorski'	6
gentianoides	1
'Gillian Blades'	4
'Gipsy Queen'	7
Golden Tiara® 'Kugotia'	9
gracilifolia var. *gracilifolia*	3
'Guernsey Cream'	4
'Hagley Hybrid'	7
'Hainton Ruby'	4
'Haku Ookan'	4
'Helen Cropper'	4
'Henryi'	6
heracleifolia var. *heracleifolia*	9
heracleifolia 'Cote d'Azur'	9
heracleifolia var. *davidiana*	9
heracleifolia var. *d.* 'Wyevale'	9
'H. F. Young'	4
hirsutissima var. *scottii*	9
'Honora'	7
'Horn of Plenty'	4
'Huldine'	9
integrifolia var. *integrifolia*	9
integrifolia 'Alba'	9
integrifolia 'Pangbourne Pink'	9
integrifolia 'Rosea'	9
'Jackmanii'	7
'Jackmanii Alba'	5
'Jackmanii Rubra'	5
'Jackmanii Superba'	7
'James Mason'	4
'Jan Pawel II'	7
japonica	1
'John Huxtable'	7
'John Warren'	4
Josephine™ 'Evijohill'®	5
× *jouiniana* 'Praecox'	9
'Kacper'	4
'Kathleen Dunford'	5
'Kathleen Wheeler'	4
'Ken Donson'	4
'King Edward VII'	4
'King George V'	4
'Kiri Te Kanawa'	5
'Königskind'	4
koreana var. *koreana*	2
koreana var. *lutea*	2

Variety	Section	Variety	Section	Variety	Section
'Lady Betty Balfour'	7	'Mrs. Hope'	6	*terniflora*	9
'Lady Caroline Nevill'	5	'Mrs James Mason'	4	*terniflora* 'Robusta'	9
'Lady Londesborough'	4	'Mrs. N. Thompson'	4	*texensis*	9
'Lady Northcliffe'	4	'Mrs. P. B. Truax'	4	*texensis* 'Duchess of Albany'	9
'Lasurstern'	4	'Mrs Robert Brydon'	9	*texensis* 'Etoile Rose'	9
'Lawsoniana'	6	'Mrs. Spencer Castle'	5	*texensis* 'Gravetye Beauty'	9
'Lemon Chiffon'	4	'Multi Blue'	5	*texensis* 'Ladybird Johnson'	9
Liberation™ 'Evifive'®	4	'Myojo'	5	*texensis* 'Pagoda'	9
ligusticifolia	9	*napaulensis*	1	*texensis* 'Princess Diana'	9
'Lilacina Floribunda'	7	'Natascha'	4	*texensis* 'Sir Trevor Lawrence'	9
'Lincoln Star'	4	'Nelly Moser'	4	'The President'	4
'Lord Nevill'	4	'Niobe'	4	'The Velvet'	4
'Louise Rowe'	5	*orientalis*	9	*tibetana* var. *tibetana*	9
macropetala var. *macropetala*	2	*paniculata* var. *paniculata*	1	*tibetana* var. *vernayi*	9
macropetala 'Alborosea'	2	*paniculata* 'Bodnant'	1	*tibetana* var. *vernayi* 'L & S' 13342	9
macropetala 'Anders'	2	*paniculata* 'Lobata'	1	'Torleif'	6
macropetala 'Ballet Skirt'	2	*patens*	4	× *triternata* 'Rubromarginata'	9
macropetala 'Blue Bird'	2	'Paul Farges' Summer Snow	9	'Twilight'	4
macropetala 'Floralia'	2	'Perle d'Azur'	7	'Ulrique'	4
macropetala 'Jan Lindmark'	2	'Perrin's Pride'	7	× *vedrariensis* 'Highdown'	3
macropetala 'Lagoon'	2	Petit Faucon™ 'Evisix'®	9	'Veronica's Choice'	5
macropetala 'Lincolnshire Lady'	2	'Peveril Pearl'	6	'Victoria'	7
macropetala 'Maidwell Hall'	2	'Pink Champagne'	4	'Ville de Lyon'	7
macropetala 'Markham's Pink'	2	'Pink Fantasy'	7	Vino™ 'Poulvo'®	4
macropetala 'Pauline'	2	*pitcheri*	9	'Violet Charm'	6
macropetala 'Rosy O'Grady'	2	*potanini* var. *fargesii*	9	*viorna*	9
macropetala 'White Moth'	2	'Prince Charles'	7	*virginiana*	9
macropetala 'White Swan'	2	'Prins Hendrik'	6	*vitalba*	9
macropetala 'White Wings'	2	'Proteus'	5	*viticella*	8
'Madame Baron Veillard'	7	'Ramona'	6	*viticella* 'Abundance'	8
'Madame Edouard André'	7	*recta* var. *recta*	9	*viticella* 'Alba Luxurians'	8
'Madame Grangé'	7	*recta* var. *purpurea*	9	*viticella* 'Betty Corning'	8
'Marcel Moser'	4	*rehderiana*	9	*viticella* 'Blue Belle'	8
'Margaret Hunt'	7	'Rhapsody'	7	*viticella* 'Carmencita'	8
'Marie Boisselot'	6	'Richard Pennell'	4	*viticella* 'Etoile Violette'	8
marmoraria	1	'Romantika'	7	*viticella* 'Kermesina'	8
'Masquerade'	4	'Rouge Cardinal'	7	*viticella* 'Little Nell'	8
'Maureen'	6	'Royalty'	5	*viticella* 'Mm. Julia Correvon'	8
meyeniana	1	Royal Velvet™ 'Evifour'®	4	*viticella* 'Margot Koster'	8
'Minister'	4	'Ruby Glow'	4	*viticella* 'Minuet'	8
'Miss Bateman'	4	'Scartho Gem'	4	*viticella* 'Polish Spirit'	8
'Miss Crawshay'	5	'Sealand Gem'	4	*viticella* 'Purpurea Plena'	8
montana var. *montana*	3	'Serenata'	6	*viticella* 'Purpurea Plena Elegans'	8
montana 'Alexandra'	3	*serratifolia*	9	*viticella* 'Royal Velours'	8
montana 'Broughton Star'	3	'Sho Un'	4	*viticella* 'Södertälje'	8
montana 'Elizabeth'	3	'Silver Moon'	4	*viticella* 'Tango'	8
montana f. *grandiflora*	3	'Sir Garnet Wolseley'	4	*viticella* 'Venosa Violacea'	8
montana 'Freda'	3	'Snow Queen'	4	Vivienne 'Beth Currie'	4
montana 'Gothenburg'	3	'Souvenir de Capitaine		'Voluceau'	7
montana 'Margaret Jones'	3	Thuilleaux'	4	'Vyvyan Pennell'	5
montana 'Marjorie'	3	'Special Occasion'	4	'Wada's Primrose'	4
montana 'Mayleen'	3	*stans*	9	'Walter Pennell'	5
montana 'Pink Perfection'	3	'Star of India'	7	'Warsaw Nike'	4
montana 'Tetrarose'	3	Sugar Candy™ 'Evione'®	4	'W. E. Gladstone'	6
montana 'Vera'	3	'Sunset'	4	'Will Goodwin'	4
montana var. *rubens*	3	'Sylvia Denny'	5	'William Kennett'	4
montana var. *r.* 'Picton's Variety'	3	*tangutica* var. *tangutica*	9	*williamsii*	1
montana var. *wilsonii*	3	*tangutica* 'Aureolin'	9		
'Moonlight'	4	*tangutica* 'Bill MacKenzie'	9		
'Mrs. Bush'	6	*tangutica* 'Burford Variety'	9		
'Mrs. Cholmondeley'	4	*tangutica* 'Helios'	9		
'Mrs. George Jackman'	5	*tangutica* var. *obtusiuscula*	9		

Pruning Group One

Sections 1, 2 & 3

Group One Pruning Instructions

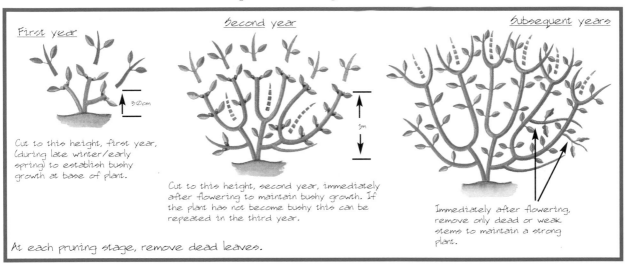

First year

Cut to this height, first year, (during late winter/early spring) to establish bushy growth at base of plant.

30cm

Second year

Cut to this height, second year, immediately after flowering to maintain bushy growth. If the plant has not become bushy this can be repeated in the third year.

1m

Subsequent years

Immediately after flowering, remove only dead or weak stems to maintain a strong plant.

At each pruning stage, remove dead leaves.

Section 1 – Evergreen and Early Flowering Species

The clematis in this section are generally only suitable for growing successfully in sheltered warm gardens in England Central and Southern Europe (hardiness zones 7-9, unless otherwise stated, see page 78) and warmer zones in the United States. However, they are also ideal for growing in a conservatory or glass-house, either in containers with the less vigorous types or, if possible, direct into the soil. In cold districts, the less hardy and less vigorous species and their forms may also be grown outside in the summer on a patio for instance and taken indoors during the approach to winter. These clematis are natives of both the southern and northern hemisphere. Follow the Group One pruning instructions for

SOME OF THE MOST REWARDING CLEMATIS TO GROW IN THIS SUB-GROUP:

armandii
armandii 'Apple Blossom'
× *cartmanii* **Avalanche**™ 'Blaaval'®
cirrhosa 'Freckles'
cirrhosa var. *balearica*
paniculata 'Bodnant'

Clematis gentianoides is not winter hardy and is most suitable for conservatory cultivation.

SPECIES OR CULTIVAR	DESCRIPTION AND OUTSTANDING FEATURES	FLOWERING SEASON IN ENGLAND (see page 78 for months)	HEIGHT
afoliata	2cm (³/₄in) long, nodding, scented, pale yellow flowers. Cream anthers. Semi-climbing, evergreen species, sprawling habit. Long, rush-like stems, no true leaves. Hardiness zone 8–9.	Early to mid spring	2.5m (8¹/₄ft)
armandii	Flat, open flowers, 4–5cm (1¹/₂–2in) across, creamy white to pure white tepals. Off-white anthers, hawthorn scent. Large, pointed leaves, bronze when young, dark green and leathery when mature. Hardiest evergreen. Needs sheltered south- or southwest-facing site under large wall, except in warmest areas. Hardiness zone 6–9.	Early to mid spring	4.5–6m (15–20ft)
armandii 'Apple Blossom'	5cm (2in) wide flowers, whitish pink tepals with pale pink reverse. Flower buds and flower stems also pink. Strong vanilla scent. Leaflets blunter, wider and slightly more bronze than the species. Hardiness zone 6–9.	Early to mid spring	4.5–6m (15–20ft)
armandii 'Jefferies'	Scented, white, 5cm (2in) wide flowers, more gappy than the species. Leaflets longer, narrower and more pointed than the species. May produce a crop of summer flowers. Hardiness zone 6–9.	Early to mid spring	5–6m (16¹/₂–20 ft)
australis	Creamy green, star-shaped, semi-nodding flowers, 2cm (³/₄in) across. Scented. New Zealand evergreen species, only partially hardy. Hardiness zone 8–9.	Early to mid spring	2m (6¹/₂ft)
× *cartmanii* Avalanche™ 'Blaaval'®	Profuse, pure white, flat open flowers, 7–8cm (2³/₄–3in) across, borne in panicles. Short dark yellow stamens, no styles. Glossy, fleshy, leathery, dark green leaves. Strong, vigorous, evergreen plant, can be pruned to keep compact. Winter hardy to –8°C (18°F).	Early to mid spring	3–4m (10–13ft)
× *cartmanii* 'Joe'	Profuse, white, semi-nodding, open cup-shaped, 2.5cm (1in) wide flowers. Coarse, fern-like, dark green foliage, non-clinging, can be trained. Hardy to –5°C (23°F). Valuable conservatory/glasshouse plant, or outside in well-drained soil & shelter.	Early to mid spring	2m (6¹/₂ft)
cirrhosa var. *cirrhosa*	Broad, bell-shaped flowers, 4cm (1¹/₂in) deep. Light greenish yellow tepals, covered in purple blotches. Attractive dark evergreen, glossy foliage.	Early to late winter	3–4m (10–13ft)
cirrhosa 'Freckles' ♛	7.5cm (3in) flowers have long, 6–7cm (2¹/₄–2³/₄in) flower stalks. Tepal base colour creamy pink, with red-maroon blotches inside. Larger leaves than species. May go into slight summer dormancy, winter hardy to –12°C (10°F)	Mid to late autumn	3–4 m (10–13ft)
cirrhosa 'Ourika Valley'	Nodding, bell-shaped flowers, 4–5cm (1¹/₂–2in) long, cream anthers. Pale yellow tepals without blotches. Vigorous plant, more free-flowering & more winter hardy than the species.	Late winter to early spring	3–4m (10–13ft)
cirrhosa 'Wisley Cream'	4cm (1¹/₂in) deep flowers, tepals greenish-cream without blotches, scented. Leaves lighter green than species, strong growing habit.	Mid winter to early spring	3–4m (10–13ft)
cirrhosa var. *balearica* ♛	Flowers narrower & longer than species, 5cm (2in) deep. Tepals slightly twisted, with red-brown blotches. Foliage turns bronze outside in winter. Less vigorous or dense in habit than species.	Mid to late winter	3m (10ft)
finetiana	Star-shaped white flowers, 4cm (1¹/₂in) wide, strongly scented. Bright green evergreen foliage. Half hardy, needs well-protected site. Hardiness zone 8–9.	Late spring to early summer	3–4m (10–13ft)
forsteri	Semi-nodding, open star-shaped flowers, 2–3cm (³/₄–1¹/₄in) wide, in large clusters. Tepals creamy lime green, strongly scented, lemon verbena. Apple green leaves, dioecious evergreen. Hardiness zone 8–9.	Mid spring	2m (6¹/₂ft)

SPECIES OR CULTIVAR	DESCRIPTION AND OUTSTANDING FEATURES	FLOWERING SEASON IN ENGLAND *(see page 78 for months)*	HEIGHT
gentianoides	White, star-shaped flowers, 2.5–4cm (1–1¹/₂in) wide, hawthorn scent. Flowers for three months, best in dry sunny position, not winter hardy. Non-clinging evergreen with coarse narrow leaves, bushy habit. Hardiness zone 8–9.	Early to mid spring	45–60cm (1¹/₂–2ft)
japonica	Nodding, bell-shaped flowers, 3cm (1¹/₄in) deep, tepals fleshy, wax-like, recurving at tips. Colour variable from maroon to pale yellow. Pale green leaves. Needs a sunny position. Hardiness zone 6–9.	Early summer	2m (6¹/₂ft)
marmoraria	Creamy white flowers, greenish when young, 2cm (³/₄in) wide, borne close to foliage. Deep glossy green leaves, dwarf evergreen, ideal for alpine house. Hardiness zone 8–9.	Early spring	10–12.5cm (4–5in)
meyeniana	Open, white or pink flowers, 2.5cm (1in) across, borne in racemes, narrow oblong tepals. Thick leaflets, evergreen, needs a sheltered position. Hardiness zone 9.	Early to mid spring	4.5–5m (15–16¹/₂ft)
napaulensis	Scented, nodding, creamy white, 2.5cm (1in) long flowers, borne in clusters. Purple-red anthers, bright green foliage. Plant goes into summer dormancy, not winter hardy. Hardiness zone 8–9.	Early to mid winter	3–4m (10–13ft)
paniculata var. *paniculata*	Semi-nodding, saucer-shaped white flowers, 5cm (2in) diameter, borne in clusters. Dioecious species, pink anthers in male forms, smaller flowers & a style in female forms. Shiny, dark green leaves, very free-flowering. Needs good drainage & sheltered, sunny position, ideal for conservatory.	Early to mid spring	3–4m (10–13ft)
paniculata 'Bodnant'	Large white flowers, 6cm (2¹/₂in) diameter, large central boss of pink stamens. Very free-flowering, foliage larger than species.	Early to mid spring	3–4m (10–13ft)
paniculata 'Lobata'	Sparsely produced white flowers, 4cm (1¹/₂in) across. Deeply lobed leaves.	Early to mid spring	2–3m (6¹/₂–10ft)
williamsii	Cream, nodding flowers, 4cm (1¹/₂in) across, with cream stamens. Pointed tepals, reflexed when mature. Foliage greyish-green in early spring, with silver central band, later leaves bright green. Deciduous. Vigorous habit. Needs well-drained, sheltered, sunny position, or under glass.	Early to mid spring	3m (10ft)

Clematis armandii is the hardiest evergreen clematis.

Section 2 – Alpina and Macropetala Types

These extremely hardy and garden worthy species are natives of the European and Chinese mountains. The European species, *alpina*, has single nodding flowers with four tepals. The Chinese species, *macropetala*, has semi-double flowers which are also nodding but are slightly more open. Both species and their cultivars flower from the old previous season's stems during spring and produce occasional summer flowers which look delightful with the seed heads from the earlier flowers. For the clematis in this section, hardiness zones 3-9 applies, unless otherwise stated (see page 78). This group is extremely winter hardy and ideal for cold exposed positions. Can be grown through trees, shrubs and wall-trained shrubs, on pergolas, archways, low fences and in containers for the patio. Attractive seed heads. Follow the Group One pruning instructions for all the clematis in this section.

SOME OF THE MOST REWARDING CLEMATIS TO GROW IN THIS SUB-GROUP:

alpina 'Constance'
alpina 'Foxy'
alpina 'Frankie'
alpina 'Pink Flamingo'
macropetala var. *macropetala*
macropetala 'Pauline'
macropetala 'Lagoon'
macropetala 'Markham's Pink
macropetala 'White Wings'

Clematis alpina 'Blue Dancer'

SPECIES OR CULTIVAR	DESCRIPTION AND OUTSTANDING FEATURES	FLOWERING SEASON IN ENGLAND *(see page 78 for months)*	HEIGHT
alpina var. *alpina*	5cm (2in) long, semi-nodding to nodding, blue to mauve flowers. Large boss of cream petaloid staminodes, outer being longer and spoon-shaped. Deciduous climber, ribbed stems.	Mid to late spring	2–3m (6^{1}/$_{2}$–10ft)
alpina 'Albiflora'	5cm (2in) long, creamy white flowers.	Mid to late spring	2.5–3m (8^{1}/$_{4}$–10ft)
alpina 'Blue Dancer'	5–7.5cm (2–3in) long, very pale blue flowers. Narrow, twisted, pointed tepals.	Mid to late spring	3m (10ft)
alpina 'Burford White'	Full flower, 5cm (2in) deep, creamy white tepals. Attractive light green foliage.	Mid to late spring	2–3m (6^{1}/$_{2}$–10ft)
alpina 'Columbine'	5cm (2in) long, very pale blue flower, pointed tepals. Pale green foliage, attractive seed heads.	Mid to late spring	2–3m (6^{1}/$_{2}$–10ft)
alpina 'Constance'	5cm (2in) deep, rich purple-pink semi-double flowers. Free-flowering, attractive seed heads.	Mid to late spring	3m (10ft)
alpina 'Cyanea'	5cm (2in) long, deep blue flower. Four inner, pointed tepals. Pleasant green foliage. Free-flowering.	Mid to late spring	2–3m (6^{1}/$_{2}$–10ft)
alpina 'Foxy'	5cm (2in) deep, very pale pink flowers, broad, pointed tepals, pretty pink inner skirt. Light green foliage, attractive seed heads. One of most free-flowering alpina cultivars.	Mid to late spring	3 m (10ft)

SPECIES OR CULTIVAR	DESCRIPTION AND OUTSTANDING FEATURES	FLOWERING SEASON IN ENGLAND (see page 78 for months)	HEIGHT
alpina 'Frankie'	Broad, mid-blue tepals, 5cm (2in) long, flowers have pretty inner skirt. Outer petaloid stamens have pale blue tips. Attractive seed heads & one of most free-flowering alpina cultivars.	Mid to late spring	3m (10ft)
alpina 'Helsingborg' ♛	Deep blue/purple flowers, 5cm (2in) long, dark purple petaloid stamens. Very free-flowering.	Mid to late spring	3m (10ft)
alpina 'Jacqueline du Pré'	Large, pale pink, semi-nodding flowers, freely borne. Tepals 5cm (2in) long, 2.5cm (1in) wide, pale maroon veins on reverse. Pale green foliage.	Mid to late spring	3m (10ft)
alpina 'Pamela Jackman'	Short, stubby, deep blue flowers, 4cm (1½in) deep.	Mid to late spring	2–3m (6½–10ft)
alpina 'Pink Flamingo'	4cm (1½in) semi-double flowers, pale pink with red veins. Long flowering season, attractive seed heads.	Mid to late spring, and mid to late summer	3m (10ft)
alpina 'Ruby'	Tepals 4–5cm (1½–2in) long, purple-pink flowers. Very strong-growing habit.	Mid spring and occasional autumn flowers	3–4m (10–13ft)
alpina 'Tage Lundell'	Tepals 4–5cm (1½–2in) long, distinctive dark rose-purple flowers.	Mid to late spring	3m (10ft)
alpina 'White Columbine' ♛	Clear white, 4–5cm (1½–2in) long, pointed tepals. Light green foliage, very free-flowering & attractive seed heads.	Mid to late spring	2–3m (6½–10ft)
alpina 'Willy'	Flowers 4–5cm (1½–2in) long, pale pink tepals, darker on outside. Vigorous habit, free-flowering.	Mid to late spring, and late summer	2–3m (6½–10ft)
alpina var. *ochotensis*	Nodding slate-blue flowers, 5cm (2in) long. Large boss of petaloid stamens. Deciduous, scrambling species.	Late spring to early summer	2m (6½ft)
alpina var. *ochotensis* 'Carmen Rose'	Purplish-pink flowers, 6–7cm (2¼–2¾in) long, outer tepals broader. Showy, free-flowering.	Late spring to early summer	3m (10ft)
alpina var. *ochotensis* 'Frances Rivis' (syn a. 'Blue Giant') ♛	Large pale blue flowers, 5–6cm (2–2¼in) long, broad, slightly twisted tepals. Very free-flowering.	Mid to late spring	3m (10ft)
alpina var. *sibirica* (syn. *sibirica*)	Clear white, open bell-shaped flowers, 5cm (2in) long, pointed tepals. Creamy white petaloid stamens. Pale green foliage. Short-growing, deciduous plant.	Late spring	2m (6½ft)
chiisanensis	Variable colour—pale yellow to brownish orange yellow – darker at base. Tepals ribbed & spurred, 5cm (2in) long. Nodding flowers, solitary or in groups of three. Hardiness zone 5-9.	Late spring to summer	2–3m (6½–10ft)
columbiana var. *tenuiloba*	Open bell-shaped flowers, 3–4cm (1¼–1½in) deep. Tepal colour from blue to purple. Semi-woody, deciduous scrambler.	Late spring	15cm (6in)

SPECIES OR CULTIVAR	DESCRIPTION AND OUTSTANDING FEATURES	FLOWERING SEASON IN ENGLAND (see page 78 for months)	HEIGHT
koreana var. *koreana*	Open bell-shaped flowers, 7.5cm (3in), solitary or in clusters. Reddish purple tepals, pointed tips. Creamy yellow petaloid staminodes. Hardiness zone 5-9.	Late spring to early summer	2–3 m (6½–10ft)
koreana var. *lutea*	Attractive yellow flowers. Hardiness zone 5-9.	Late spring to early summer	2–3 m (6½–10ft)
macropetala var. *macropetala*	Pendulous, open bell-shaped, blue to violet-blue flowers, 4–5cm (1½–2in) long. Numerous staminodes, outer–blue, inner–bluish-white to white, flowers appear double. Abundant attractive seed heads, becoming fluffy. Extremely winter hardy even in exposed situations.	Mid to late spring	2.5–3m (8¼–10ft)
macropetala 'Alborosea'	Lantern-like flowers 6cm (2¼in) long. Outer tepals pinkish-mauve, inner petaloid staminodes lighter.	Mid to late spring	3m (10ft)
macropetala 'Anders'	4–5cm (1½–2in) long, lavender-blue flowers. A good cultivar.	Mid to late spring	2–3m (6½–10ft)
macropetala 'Ballet Skirt'	Fully double, large 6cm (2¼in) deep flowers. Deep pinkish tepals and petaloid staminodes. Not as vigorous as other cultivars.	Mid to late spring	2.5m (8¼ft)

Clementis alpina 'Pink Flamingo' has delightful semi-double flowers.

Clematis macropetala 'Pauline', a good new cultivar.

SPECIES OR CULTIVAR	DESCRIPTION AND OUTSTANDING FEATURES	FLOWERING SEASON IN ENGLAND (*see page 78 for months*)	HEIGHT
macropetala 'Blue Bird'	Gappy flower, 6cm (2¼in) deep. Slim, twisted mauve-blue outer tepals, petaloid staminodes paler, creamy white in centre. Vigorous plant.	Mid to late spring, with some summer flowers	3m (10ft)
macropetala 'Floralia'	Stubby 4cm (1½ in) long, pale blue flowers on purple-red flower stalks.	Mid to late spring	2.5m (8¼ft)
macropetala 'Jan Lindmark'	Mauve-purple 4cm (1½ in) long flowers. Outer tepals slightly twisted. Earliest flowering of alpina or macropetala types. Foliage may become untidy.	Mid to late spring	2.5m (8¼ft)
macropetala 'Lagoon'	Large, spiky, very deep blue flowers, 6cm (2¼in) deep. The darkest of all blue cultivars, best with a light background. Later flowering than most macropetala types.	Mid to late spring	2–3m (6½–10ft)
macropetala 'Lincolnshire Lady'	Fully double nodding flowers, 4–7cm (1½–2¾in) long. Dusky blue outer tepals in two obvious pairs. Paler, long, thin inner tepals.	Mid to late spring, with occasional summer flowers	3m (10ft)
macropetala 'Maidwell Hall' ♟	Pale blue to lavender, fully double, semi-nodding flowers, 5cm (2in) deep. Some plants sold under this name have deep blue flowers.	Mid to late spring	2.5m (8¼ft)
macropetala 'Markham's Pink' ♟	Fully double, deep pink flowers, 5cm (2 in) long, free-flowering. Pale green foliage.	Mid to late spring	3m (10ft)
macropetala 'Pauline'	Extra large, 5–7cm (2–2¾in) long flowers. Mid to dark blue, long, pointed outer tepals with attractive skirt of petaloid staminodes. Free-flowering plant, strong-growing.	Mid to late spring	3m (10ft)
macropetala 'Rosy O'Grady'	Spiky, open flowers, 5–7cm (2–2¾in) long. Pinky-mauve outer tepals, inner skirt lighter in colour. Strong-growing.	Mid to late spring	3m (10ft)
macropetala 'White Moth' (syn *alpina* ssp. *sibirica* 'White Moth')	Creamy white stubby flowers, 3–4cm (1¼–1½in) long. Outer tepals spread when mature. Pale green foliage, not very vigorous but ideal for a small garden, attractive seed heads. Latest of alpina or macropetala types to flower.	Late spring	2m (6½ft)
macropetala 'White Swan'	Creamy white, fully double, semi-nodding flowers, 5–6cm (2–2¼in) long. Good pale green foliage. Slow to establish.	Late spring	2m (6½ft)
macropetala 'White Wings'	Creamy white, fully double flowers, 5–6cm (2–2¼in) long. Pale green foliage. Very free-flowering, best of the white macropetala types.	Late spring	2–3m (6½–10ft)

Section 3 – Montana Types

Clematis montana, a Himalayan species, and its forms, are most useful garden plants for covering unsightly walls, old buildings, etc. Their use seems endless. They can be expected to grow 6-11 metres, or even higher if conditions for growth are favourable. As well as covering walls, they also lend themselves to enhancing large evergreen trees such as straggly old pine trees and large conifers. This group flowers from the ripened previous season's stems, mainly in late spring to early summer, but also produces a few summer flowers. Follow the Group One pruning instructions for all the clematis in this section. Hardiness zone 7–9 applies unless otherwise stated (see page 78).

SOME OF THE MOST REWARDING CLEMATIS TO GROW IN THIS SUB-GROUP:

montana 'Broughton Star'
montana 'Elizabeth'
montana f. *grandiflora*
montana 'Freda'
montana 'Mayleen'
montana 'Tetrarose'

Clematis montana 'Tetrarose'

SPECIES OR CULTIVAR	DESCRIPTION AND OUTSTANDING FEATURES	FLOWERING SEASON IN ENGLAND *(see page 78 for months)*	HEIGHT
chrysocoma	Pink or white, flat flowers, cup-shaped when young, 5cm (2in) diameter. Large boss of short yellow stamens. Stems, leaf stalks & leaflets downy, covered in brownish-yellow hairs. Semi-hardy, needs free-draining soil. Hardiness zone 8–9.	Early to late summer	2m (6½ft)
chrysocoma 'Continuity'	5cm (2in) wide flowers on long flower stalk, 20cm (8in). Tepals mid-pale pink, darker pink reverse, satin texture & blunt tips. Long filaments, deep yellow anthers. Needs well-drained soil in sheltered position. Not winter hardy but can be grown under cover. Hardiness zone 8–9.	Early to late summer	2m (6½ft)
chrysocoma hybrid	Pale pink cup-shaped flowers, 4–5cm (1½–2in) across, yellow anthers. Leaflets large, thick & hairy, dark green to bronze.	Late spring	5m (16½ft)
gracilifolia var. *gracilifolia*	White, open flowers, 5cm (2in) across, rather gappy. Attractive foliage, leaves hairy. Hardiness zone 6–9	Mid to late spring	5m (16½ft)
montana var. *montana*	Gappy, flat, open white flowers, 5cm (2in) wide, occasional summer flowers. Not fully winter hardy in very cold climates. Very vigorous.	Late spring to early summer	8m (26ft)
montana 'Alexander'	Large, fully-rounded open flowers, 6cm (2¼in) across, creamy anthers. Leaves larger than species & a good green colour. Needs full sun to flower well.	Late spring to early summer	8m (26ft)

SPECIES OR CULTIVAR	DESCRIPTION AND OUTSTANDING FEATURES	FLOWERING SEASON IN ENGLAND (see page 78 for months)	HEIGHT
montana 'Broughton Star' B C S C of M 1998	Unusual semi-double to fully double cup-shaped flowers, 4–7cm (1½–2¾in) across. Deep dusky pink tepals with darker veins. Interesting trifoliate leaves, deeply serrated, bronze when young, dark green when mature. Prefers a sunny position. Good cut flower for small arrangements.	Late spring to early summer	4–5m (13–16½ft)
montana 'Elizabeth'	Slightly gappy, 6cm (2¼in) wide flowers with long filaments & spiky anthers. Tepals pale pink with a satiny sheen. Vanilla scent. Bronze foliage matures to green.	Late spring to early summer	8–10m (26–33ft)
montana f. *grandiflora*	Freely produced, clear white, 7.5cm (3in) diameter flowers. Dark green foliage. Very strong-growing & vigorous, ideal for covering large areas. Hardiest montana type. Hardiness zone 6–9.	Late spring to early summer	10–11m (33–36ft)
montana 'Freda'	5cm (2in) flowers, deep pink with dark pink/red margins & contrasting yellow anthers. Very deep bronze foliage. Compact plant, suitable for small gardens.	Late spring to early summer	6–8m (20–26ft)
montana 'Gothenburg'	Creamy pink rounded flowers, 4–6cm (1½–2¼in) across, on long flower stalks. Prominent creamy anthers. Attractive foliage, bronze with a central silver band.	Late spring to early summer	5m (16½ft)
montana 'Margaret Jones'	Semi-double star-shaped flowers, 5cm (2in) across. Creamy-green white long, thin outer tepals, inner ring of smaller, shorter petaloid staminodes. Stamens absent, style green. Needs sunny south or south-west position.	Late spring to early summer	4.5m (15ft)

Clematis montana f grandiflora produces hundreds of flowers.

SPECIES OR CULTIVAR	DESCRIPTION AND OUTSTANDING FEATURES	FLOWERING SEASON IN ENGLAND (see page 78 for months)	HEIGHT
montana 'Marjorie'	Semi-double 6cm (2¼in) diameter flowers. In cold spring, tepals open greenish pink, turning creamy pink in sunlight. Needs full sun.	Late spring to early summer	8m (26ft)
montana 'Mayleen'	Fully rounded 6cm (2¼in) diameter flowers, strong vanilla scent. Satiny pink tepals, yellow anthers, bronze foliage.	Late spring to early summer	8–10m (26–33ft)
montana 'Pink Perfection'	Rounded pink flowers, 6cm (2¼in) across, yellow anthers & bronze foliage. Good vanilla scent. Strong-growing plant.	Late spring to early summer	8–10m (26–33ft)
montana 'Tetrarose' 🏆	Large, cup-shaped flowers, 7.5cm (3in) wide. Thick tepals, deep rosy-mauve with a stain sheen. Deep yellow stamens. Large, bronze green leaves maturing to deep bronze purple.	Late spring to early summer	8m (26ft)
montana 'Vera'	Deep pink, 5–7cm (2–2¾in) wide flowers, pleasant vanilla scent. Large bronze green leaves, very strong-growing plant	Late spring to early summer	10m (33ft)
montana var. *rubens* 🏆	Coloured form of the species with rosy-red flowers, 5cm (2in) diameter, bronze foliage. Variable forms on sale, original lost to cultivation.	Late spring to early summer	8–10m (26–33ft)
montana var. *rubens* 'Picton's Variety'	Deep mauve pink, 5cm (2in) wide flowers. Usually four tepals, occasional midsummer flowers have six. Compact plant with bronzy foliage.	Late spring to early summer, occasional midsummer flowers	4.5m (15ft)
montana var. *wilsonii*	Creamy white flowers, 5cm (2in), borne on long flower stalks, large boss of cream stamens. Leaves more fleshy than species. Hardiness zone 6–9.	Mid to late summer	10m (33ft)
× *vedrariensis* 'Highdown'	Slightly cup-shaped, pink flowers, 5cm (2in) diameter, yellow anthers. Downy foliage, vigorous.	Late spring to early summer	6m (20ft)

Clematis montana var. wilsonii is very late flowering.

Clematis montana 'Mayleen' has bronzy foliage and strongly scented flowers.

Pruning Group Two

Sections 4, 5 & 6

Group Two Pruning Instructions

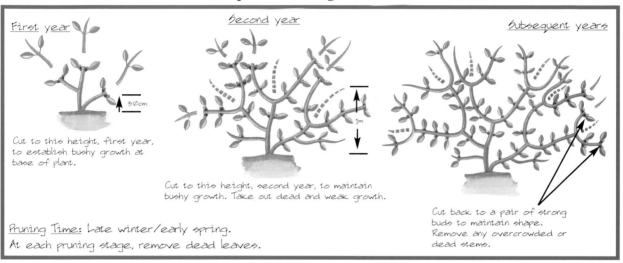

First year

Cut to this height, first year, to establish bushy growth at base of plant.

30cm

Second year

Cut to this height, second year, to maintain bushy growth. Take out dead and weak growth.

1m

Subsequent years

Cut back to a pair of strong buds to maintain shape. Remove any overcrowded or dead stems.

Pruning Time: Late winter/early spring.
At each pruning stage, remove dead leaves.

Section 4 – Early Large-Flowered Cultivars

The clematis in this section form one of the most important groups. Their habit and flowering performance give the imaginative gardener many opportunities. Most of them will grow and flower well in any aspect and they are ideal for growing through other wall trained trees and shrubs, or free standing shrubs. They have a good range of colours, their seed heads are attractive, both flowers and seed heads can be used in flower arrangements. All types can be grown in containers for the patio or conservatory garden. The flowering habit of most of the clematis in this section is also long; having flowered in late spring and early summer from the stems ripened the previous season, a second crop of flowers can be enjoyed during late summer, given good cultivation. Hardiness zone 4–9, unless otherwise stated (see page 78). Follow the Group Two pruning instructions for all the clematis in this section.

SOME OF THE MOST REWARDING CLEMATIS TO GROW IN THIS SUB-GROUP:

Anna Louise™ 'Evithree'®
'Bees' Jubilee'
Blue Moon™ 'Evirin'®
'Dr Ruppel'
'Elsa Späth'
'Gillian Blades'
'Guernsey Cream'
'H. F. Young'
'Ken Donson'
'Lady Northcliffe'
'Lasurstern'

'Miss Bateman'
'Mrs Cholmondely'
'Nelly Moser'
'Niobe'
RoyalVelvet™ 'Evifour'®
'Snow Queen'
Sugar Candy™ 'Evione'®
'Sunset'
'Warsaw Nike'
'Will Goodwin'

SPECIES OR CULTIVAR	DESCRIPTION AND OUTSTANDING FEATURES	FLOWERING SEASON IN ENGLAND (see page 78 for months)	HEIGHT
Alabast™ 'Poulala'®	12–15cm (4³/₄–6in) wide, well-formed round flowers in late spring. Mid to late summer flowers, 9cm (3¹/₂in). Tepals greenish cream, anthers creamy-yellow. For best flower colour, grow out of full sun. Slightly glaucous foliage.	Late spring to early summer, and late summer	3m (10ft)
'Anna'	Rosy-pink fully rounded, 15cm (6in) flowers, red anthers. Early flowers may be greenish-pink. Compact, free-flowering cultivar, best in a sunny position.	Late spring to early summer, and late summer	2.5m (8¹/₄ft)
Anna Louise™ 'Evithree'®	Violet flowers, 15cm (6in) wide, with reddish-brown anthers. Tepals have contrasting reddish-purple central bar. Compact free-flowering plant, ideal for containers & cut flowers.	Late spring to early autumn	2.5m (8¹/₄ft)
'Asao'	Deep pink flowers, deepest colour at tepal edges, 15cm (6in) wide, yellow anthers. Bronze foliage in late spring. Very compact, free-flowering in spring, ideal for containers.	Late spring to early summer, and late summer	2.5m (8¹/₄ft)
'Barbara Dibley'	Open flowers, 18cm (7in) across, pointed tepals, red anthers. Early flowers—deep petunia red, later flowers—much paler, thinner in texture. Medium-sized seed heads with curly seed tails. Best on west- or east-facing position.	Late spring to early summer, and late summer	2.5–3m (8¹/₄–10ft)
'Barbara Jackman'	12–15cm (4³/₄–6in) open flowers, yellow anthers. Mauve tepals with petunia-coloured central bar, fade in strong sunlight. Best on west- or east-facing position, good cut flowers.	Late spring to early summer, and late summer	2.5–3m (8¹/₄–10ft)

Clematis 'Asao', a Japanese cultivar introduced in the early 1980s.

SPECIES OR CULTIVAR	DESCRIPTION AND OUTSTANDING FEATURES	FLOWERING SEASON IN ENGLAND (see page 78 for months)	HEIGHT
'Bees' Jubilee' ♔	Open flowers, 15cm (6in) wide, light brownish anthers. Mauve-pink tepals with much deeper central bar. Medium-sized spherical seed heads. Compact plant, ideal for containers.	Spring to late summer	2.5–3m (8¼–10ft)
Blue Moon™ 'Evirin'®	Early flowers – white suffused with pale lilac, darker at edges,15–18cm (6–7in) across. Later flowers – darker & smaller, 10cm (4in). Tepals have wavy edges, anthers dark red, attractive seed heads. Compact free-flowering plant, ideal for containers, small gardens, & a very good cut flower.	Late spring to early summer, and late summer to early autumn	2.5–3m (8¼–10ft)
'Burma Star'	Fully-formed 11.5–12.5cm (4½–5in) wide flowers. Tepals very deep rich purple-blue with red highlights, dark red anthers. Compact, free-flowering plant, ideal for containers.	Late spring to early summer	2.5m (8¼ft)
'Carnaby'	Flowers 11.5–12.5cm (4½–5in) across, anthers red. Tepals deep pink with a darker bar, paler in late summer. Compact, free-flowering plant, ideal for containers.	Late spring to early summer, and late summer to early autumn	2.5m (8¼ft)
'Caroline'	Neat, terminal flowers, 9–11.5cm (3½–4½in) across. Tepals closely overlapping, with occasional thin inner tepals. Pale dusky pink with a darker central bar at the tepal base & a thin darker edge. Pale pink reverse, yellow anthers & prominent styles. Small, coarse leaves of 3–5 leaflets with crinkled edges. Compact, neat habit, ideal for small garden. Best grown out of direct sun to avoid excessive fading.	Early summer to mid summer, and late summer	2m (6½ft)
'Charissima'	Large flowers, 15–18cm (6–7in) across, dark maroon anthers. Pointed tepals, cerise with deeper bar & deeper-coloured veins throughout. Free-flowering, good cut flower.	Late spring to early summer	2.5–3m (8¼–10ft)
'Corona'	10–15cm (4–6in) wide flowers, borne profusely in spring. Tepals light purple-pink, anthers red, late summer flowers paler & fewer. Medium-sized spherical seed heads. Compact plant.	Late spring to early summer, and late summer	2m (6½ft)
'Dawn'	Fully-formed, 12cm (4¾in) wide flowers with deep red anthers. Tepals pearly white, suffused with pink, fading in strong sunlight. Bronze foliage in spring. Slightly more winter hardy than most old-wood flowering clematis. Medium-sized spherical seed heads. Very compact, free-flowering plant, ideal for containers. Suitable as cut flowers.	Late spring to early summer, and late summer	2m (6½ft)
'Dorothy Tolver'	15cm (6in) wide flowers, overlapping, pointed tepals with rounded, lightly crimpled edges. Satiny tepals mauve at base, heavily overlaid with deep mauve-pink. Bright buttercup-yellow anthers.	Late spring to early summer, and early to mid autumn	2.5–4m (8¼–13ft)
'Dr Ruppel' ♔	15cm (6in) wide flowers with light brown anthers. Tepals deep rose pink with a much deeper central bar. Large spherical seed heads with curly seed tails. Very good, compact, very free-flowering plant, one of the best for containers. Suitable as cut flowers.	Late spring to early summer, and late summer to early autumn	2.5–3m (8¼–10ft)
'Edith' ♔	12cm (4¾in) wide flowers with dark red anthers. Tepals white with green central bar in late spring. Medium-sized spherical seed heads. Very compact, ideal for containers. Suitable as cut flowers.	Late spring to early summer, and late summer	2m (6½ft)

SPECIES OR CULTIVAR	DESCRIPTION AND OUTSTANDING FEATURES	FLOWERING SEASON IN ENGLAND (see page 78 for months)	HEIGHT
'Edouard Desfossé'	12cm (4¾in) wide flowers with red anthers. Tepals pale blue with a slightly darker bar. Small, rounded seed heads. Very compact plant, very free-flowering in spring, ideal for containers.	Late spring to early summer	2m (6½ft)
'Elgar'	Single to almost semi-double flowers, 15–20cm (6–8in) across. Tepals blue-mauve, reddish when young, reflexed pointed tips, slightly floppy. Tepal reverse–whitish central band with purple ribs & mauvish-blue edge. Yellow anthers with pale mauve filaments & prominent styles. Large leaflets with pointed tips. Compact plant, free-flowering habit.	Late spring to early summer, and late summer	2–3m (6½–10ft)
'Elsa Späth' 🏆	Rounded, 15–18cm (6–7in) wide flowers, deep red anthers. Tepals mid blue, darker when first open. Rewarding, free-flowering, strong-growing plant, blooms over a long period. Good cut flower.	Late spring to early autumn	2.5–3m (8¼–10ft)
'Etoile de Paris'	12.5cm (5in) flowers, mauve-blue, very pointed tepals, red anthers. Large seed heads with neat sphere of seed tails. Very compact plant, ideal for containers, free-flowering in late spring.	Late spring to early summer	2m (6½ft)
Evening Star™ 'Evista'®	Very large flowers, 20cm (8in) across, suitable for large flower arrangements. Broad, wavy-edged tepals overlap when young but twist with age. Plummy-mauve, fading quickly to mauve, deep cerise bar. Tepal reverse has three purple-red veins down central midrib. Large boss of golden-yellow anthers, prominent pinkish-yellow styles. Strong-growing plant, suitable for containers but in shelter due to flower size.	Early summer to late summer	3m (10ft)
'Fair Rosamund'	12.5–15cm (5–6in) wide flowers with dark red anthers. Violet scented. White tepals with pale pink central bar fading gently. Compact plant.	Late spring to early summer	2m (6½ft)
'Fireworks' 🏆	Large, 18–20cm (7–8in) wide flowers in late spring & early summer. 12.5–15cm (5–6in) wide flowers in late summer. Tepals mauve-blue with very deep petunia-red bar, dark red anthers. Vigorous plant once established, with dramatic flowers suitable for arrangements.	Late spring to early summer, and late summer to early autumn	3m (10ft)
'Fujimusume'	Freely produced, 10–12.5cm (4–5in) wide flowers, powdery blue tepals, yellow anthers. Compact plant, ideal for containers.	Late spring to early summer, and late summer to early autumn	2.5m (8¼ft)
'Gillian Blades' 🏆	12.5–15cm (5–6in) wide flowers have creamy white anthers. Pointed white tepals have wavy edges. Very free-flowering, attractive seed heads. Compact plant, ideal for containers & for cut flowers.	Early summer to late summer	2.5m (8¼ft)
'Guernsey Cream'	Well-formed, full, creamy-yellow, 12.5cm (5in) wide flowers. Late summer flowers 7.5cm (3in) & paler. Tepals overlap, anthers yellow. Compact plant, free-flowering in late spring, ideal for containers & cut flowers.	Late spring to early summer, and late summer	2.5m (8¼ft)
'Hainton Ruby'	15cm (6in) wide flowers, gappy at base, red anthers. Tepals ruby-red with purple highlights, tips recurved. Broad leaflets. Strong-growing, repeat-flowering plant.	Late spring to early summer, and late summer to early autumn	3m (10ft)
'Haku Ookan'	15cm (6in) wide flowers with yellow-white anthers. Violet-blue, overlapping tepals with pointed tips. Small, well-formed, spherical seed heads. Very free-flowering, compact plant, ideal for containers & for cut flowers.	Late spring to early summer, and late summer	2.5m (8¼ft)

SPECIES OR CULTIVAR		DESCRIPTION AND OUTSTANDING FEATURES	FLOWERING SEASON IN ENGLAND (see page 78 for months)	HEIGHT
'Helen Cropper'		Mottled flowers, 15–18cm (6–7in) wide, overlapping tepals with wavy edges. Tepals dusky pink, darker central band when young, colour deeper towards edges. Creamy-white filaments, red anthers.	Late spring to early summer, and late summer	2–3m (6½–10ft)
'H. F. Young'	🏆	Wedgwood blue, 12.5–15cm (5–6in) wide flowers with pale yellow anthers. Well-formed, spherical seed heads, seed tails arranged in swirls. The most compact, free-flowering cultivar, ideal for containers.	Late spring to early summer, and late summer	2m (6½ft)
'Horn of Plenty'	🏆	Early flowers, 18cm (7in) wide; late flowers more plentiful, 10–12.5cm (4–5in), paler. Overlapping tepals rosy-mauve with deeper central bar & crinkled edges, red anthers. Good seed heads & cut flowers. Compact plant, very free-flowering in both early & late summer, ideal in containers.	Late spring to early summer, and late summer	2–3m (6½–10ft)
'James Mason'		Well-formed, white flowers, 10–12.5cm (4–5in) wide, dark red anthers.	Late spring to early summer, and late summer	2.5–3m (8¼–10ft)
'John Warren'		Very large flower, up to 23cm (9in) wide, with very pointed, overlapping tepals. Tepals French grey with three carmine bars & deep carmine edges. Red anthers. Flowers may be damaged by very strong winds.	Late spring to early summer, and late summer to early autumn	2.5–3m (8¼–10ft)

Clematis 'Mrs Cholmondeley', a reliable old cultivar which flowers over a long season.

SPECIES OR CULTIVAR	DESCRIPTION AND OUTSTANDING FEATURES	FLOWERING SEASON IN ENGLAND (see page 78 for months)	HEIGHT
'Kacper'	Very large, full flower, 23cm (9in) wide, red anthers & clear white filaments. Wavy edged tepals, deep mauve/blue/purple with deeper central band, fading gradually. Tepal reverse has broad central band of white with mauve margins. Large, dark green, pointed leaflets. Strong-looking, compact plant, ideal for a container but in shelter.	Late spring to early summer, and late summer to early autumn	2.5m (8¼ft)
'Kathleen Wheeler'	Very large early flowers, up to 23cm (9in) across, good crop of late flowers. Plummy-purple tepals fade gently. Golden yellow anthers. Attractive seed heads, good cut flower. Flowers may be damaged by very strong winds.	Late spring to early summer, and late summer to early autumn	2.5–3m (8¼–10ft)
'Ken Donson' 🏆	Well-formed flowers, 18cm (7in) across, golden-yellow anthers. Deep blue, overlapping tepals. Excellent spherical seed heads, seed tails arranged very neatly. Handsome large foliage, good cut flowers.	Late spring to early summer, and late summer	2.5–3m (8¼–10ft)
'King Edward VII'	15cm (6in) flowers, light brown anthers, later flowers may be thin in texture. Lilac-mauve tepals, pink central bar, sometimes white tips. Early flowers may be greenish. Compact, free-flowering plant.	Late spring to early summer, and late summer	2.5m (8¼ft)
'King George V'	15cm (6in) wide flowers, chocolate-coloured anthers. Pale pink, mottled tepals, much darker central bar, pointed tips. Shy-flowering cultivar, occasionally produces semi-double flowers.	Early to midsummer	2.5m (8¼ft)
'Königskind'	Cup-shaped flowers, 9–11cm (3½–4¼in) across. Mauve-blue, overlapping tepals, broad, lighter-coloured central band, attractive veining. Red anthers, prominent white styles. Very compact, very free-flowering plant, ideal for small gardens.	Late spring to early autumn	2m (6½ft)
'Lady Londesborough'	Mauve-blue, fully-rounded flowers, 12.5–15cm (5–6in) across, red anthers. Slight violet scent. Very compact plant, free-flowering in spring.	Late spring to early summer, and late summer	2m (6½ft)
'Lady Northcliffe'	Wedgwood blue flowers, 12cm (4¾in) across. Greenish-yellow anthers may have black tips. Very good, compact plant, ideal for containers/ small gardens, free-flowering over a long period.	Early summer to late summer, and early autumn	2m (6½ft)
'Lasurstern' 🏆	18cm (7in) wide flowers, deep lavender blue, yellow anthers, good cut flowers. Tepals overlapping & wavy-edged. Large, attractive, neatly-formed, spherical seed heads. Compact but vigorous habit, ideal for containers.	Late spring to early summer, and late summer to early autumn	2.5–3m (8¼–10ft)
'Lemon Chiffon'	Neat open flowers, 10–14cm (4–5½in) wide, yellow anthers. Rounded, overlapping tepals, pale yellow-cream with hint of pale purple-pink. Small, rounded leaflets. Compact habit, will grow in shade but early flowers may open green.	Late spring to early summer, and early autumn	2–3m (6½–10ft)
Liberation™ 'Evifive'®	Early flowers huge, 23cm (9in), later flowers smaller & more gappy. Deep pink, pointed tepals, deep cerise central band. Contrasting golden-yellow anthers, pinkish-grey filaments. Strong-growing cultivar.	Late spring to early summer, and late summer to early autumn	3m (10ft)
'Lincoln Star'	15cm (6in) wide flowers, raspberry-pink pointed tepals with much deeper bar, red anthers. Late summer flowers paler, best out of full sun, good cut flower.	Late spring to early summer, and late summer to early autumn	2.5–3m (8¼–10ft)

The compact habit of Clematis 'Masquerade', left and Clematis 'Snow Queen' right, makes them both ideal clematis for container growing.

SPECIES OR CULTIVAR	DESCRIPTION AND OUTSTANDING FEATURES	FLOWERING SEASON IN ENGLAND (see page 78 for months)	HEIGHT
'Lord Nevill' ♔	15cm (6in) wide, deep blue flowers, deep red anthers, flowers fade gently. Overlapping tepals with wavy edges.	Late spring to early summer, and late summer	2.5–3m (8¼–10ft)
'Marcel Moser'	Star-shaped, 15–18cm (6–7in) wide flowers, red anthers. Mauve tepals with darker central bar. Small, neat, spherical seed heads.	Early summer and mid summer	2.5–3m (8¼–10ft)
'Masquerade'	18cm (7in) wide flowers, dark red anthers. Pointed tepals, mauvish-blue with mauve central band, later flowers paler. Compact habit, free-flowering early & late, ideal for containers & cut flowers.	Late spring to early summer, and late summer to early autumn	3m (10ft)
'Minister'	Fully-rounded flowers, 13–15cm (5¼–6in) wide. Overlapping, red-purple tepals fading to mauve, greenish central midrib on reverse. Yellow anthers on red filaments, prominent styles. Compact, free-flowering plant, ideal for small gardens.	Early summer, and late summer to early autumn	2m (6½ft)
'Miss Bateman' ♔	Fully-rounded 12.5–15cm (5–6in) wide clear white flowers. Red anthers, slight scent of violets. Medium-sized, well-formed, spherical seed heads. Compact, free-flowering habit, ideal for containers & small gardens. Suitable as cut flowers.	Late spring to early summer, and late summer to early autumn	2m (6½ft)

SPECIES OR CULTIVAR	DESCRIPTION AND OUTSTANDING FEATURES	FLOWERING SEASON IN ENGLAND (see page 78 for months)	HEIGHT
'Moonlight' (syn. 'Yellow Queen')	18cm (7in) wide, creamy-yellow flowers, yellow anthers, slight scent of violets. Overlapping tepals become slightly twisted with age. Small to medium, very elegantly spherical seed heads. Undulating leaf margins. Shy grower but vigorous once established.	Late spring to early summer, and late summer	2.5m (8¼ft)
'Mrs Cholmondeley' 🏆	Very large, 18cm (7in) wide, gappy flowers. Light lavender-blue tepals, light chocolate-coloured anthers. Medium-sized, rather spiky seed heads. Free-flowering over a long period, good cut flower.	Late spring to early autumn	2.5–3m (8¼–10ft)
'Mrs James Mason'	Fully-rounded flower, 15–18cm (6–7in) across, yellow anthers. Broad, overlapping blue-mauve tepals with light purple central bar. Strong growing, suitable for a container & as a cut flower.	Late spring to early summer, and late summer to early autumn	2.5–3m (8¼–10ft)
'Mrs N Thompson'	12.5–15cm (5–6in) wide flowers, red anthers, free-flowering in early season. Tepals bluish-purple with dark petunia central band. Very compact plant, ideal for small gardens & containers.	Late spring to early summer, and late summer	2.5m (8¼ft)
'Mrs P B Truax'	Periwinkle-blue 12.5cm (5in) wide flowers, pale yellow anthers. Smallish, well-formed, spherical seed heads. Compact, very early flowering, ideal for small gardens & containers.	Late spring to early summer, and late summer	2m (6½ft)

Clematis 'William Kennett', a delightful, reliable old cultivar.

Plant Clematis 'Warsaw Nike' against a light background to show off flower colour.

SPECIES OR CULTIVAR	DESCRIPTION AND OUTSTANDING FEATURES	FLOWERING SEASON IN ENGLAND (see page 78 for months)	HEIGHT
'Myojo'	12.5–15cm (5–6in) wide flowers, prominant central boss of golden anthers. Violet-purple tepals with a darker bar. Compact habit, ideal for small gardens.	Late spring to early summer, and late summer	2.5–3m (8¼–10ft)
'Natascha'	Flowers 12–14cm (4¾–5½in) wide, prominent red anthers & pinkish-red filaments. Mauve-blue pointed tepals recurve as mature, colour fading pleasantly. White central band & mauve margins to tepal reverse. Compact, free-flowering plant, ideal for small gardens.	Late spring to early summer, and late summer	2.5m (8¼ft)
'Nelly Moser' 🏆	Cartwheel-like 15–18cm (6–7in) wide flowers, red anthers. Pale mauve pointed tepals, deeper lilac central bar. Large, well-formed, spherical seed heads. Fades in strong sunlight, does very well in full shade. Free-flowering, good for cut flowers & containers.	Late spring to early summer, and late summer to early autumn	2.5–3m (8¼–10ft)
'Niobe' 🏆	15cm (6in) wide flowers, yellow anthers. Deep red tepals become very dark in hot climates. Free-flowering over a long period, ideal for containers & cut flowers.	Late spring to early autumn	2.5–3m (8¼–10ft)
patens	This species is one of the main parents of all clematis in this section. Blue to white flowers, 10–12.5cm (4–5in) diameter, red or yellow anthers. Compact habit, ideal in a container.	Late spring to early summer	2m (6½ft)
'Pink Champagne' (syn. 'Kakio')	Full flower, 15cm (6in) wide, compact yellow anthers, prominent style. Purplish-pink, overlapping tepals, darker at margins. Medium-sized, spherical seed heads. Compact plant, free-flowering in spring, ideal for containers.	Late spring to early summer, and late summer to early autumn	2.5m (8¼ft)
'Richard Pennell'	Full flower, 15–18cm (6–7in) wide, golden-yellow anthers, red filaments. Rich purple-blue, overlapping tepals fade gently. Good cut flowers.	Early summer to late summer, and early autumn	2.5–3m (8¼–10ft)
RoyalVelvet™ 'Evifour'®	Rich velvet-purple flowers, 15cm (6in) wide, dark red anthers. Slightly bronze-coloured foliage in spring. Extremely free-flowering plant, compact habit, ideal for small gardens & containers. Good cut flowers.	Late spring to early autumn	2.5m (8¼ft)
'Ruby Glow'	15–18cm (6–7in) wide flowers, rosy-mauve with a ruby glow, red anthers. Compact plant, very free-flowering in spring, plus good crop of later flowers. Ideal for small gardens & containers, good cut flowers.	Late spring to early autumn	2.5m (8¼ft)
'Scartho Gem'	15–18cm (6–7in) wide flowers, light pinkish-brown anthers. Bright pink, overlapping, wavy-edged tepals, much deeper-coloured central band. Later flowers paler & smaller, 15cm (6in). Ideal for containers & cut flowers.	Late spring to early summer, and late summer	2.5m (8¼ft)
'Sealand Gem'	12.5cm (5in) wide flowers, light brown anthers. Lavender tepals with dark pink central bar. Not very free-flowering.	Early to late summer	3m (10ft)
'Sho Un'	Fully-rounded, 18cm (7in) wide flower, yellow anthers. Overlapping tepals, blue with purple highlights. Strong-growing plant.	Early summer to early autumn	2.5–3m (8¼–10ft)
'Silver Moon' 🏆	Very full flower, 15cm (6in) across, creamy-white anthers. Unusual-coloured, silvery-mauve, overlapping tepals. Very compact, free-flowering in early season, ideal for small gardens & containers.	Late spring to early summer, and late summer	2m (6½ft)

SPECIES OR CULTIVAR	DESCRIPTION AND OUTSTANDING FEATURES	FLOWERING SEASON IN ENGLAND (see page 78 for months)	HEIGHT
'Sir Garnet Wolseley'	Fully-rounded 12.5–15cm (5–6in) wide flowers, red anthers. Slight violet scent. Mauve-blue tepals fade gently. The earliest large-flowered clematis to flower. Compact, free-flowering in early season, ideal for small gardens.	Late spring to early summer, and late summer	2.5m (8¼ft)
'Snow Queen'	Large, well-formed early flowers, 15–18cm (6–7in) across, red anthers. Plenty of later flowers, 10cm (4in) across. White tepals tinged with pale pink, sometimes with very pale blue. Compact habit, ideal for containers. Good cut flower.	Late spring to early summer, and late summer to early autumn	2.5m (8¼ft)
'Souvenir du Capitaine Thuilleaux'	Fully-rounded 15cm (6in) wide flowers, dark red anthers. Creamy-pink tepals with deeper pink bands and crinkled edges. Compact habit, ideal for containers & small gardens. Very free-flowering in early season.	Late spring to early summer, and late summer	2m (6½ft)
'Special Occasion'	10–12.5cm (4–5in) wide flowers, light brown anthers. Pale bluish-pink, rounded tepals, lighter in centre. Compact habit.	Early summer to midsummer	2m (6½ft)
Sugar Candy™ 'Evione'®	15–18cm (6–7in) wide flowers, yellow anthers with grey filaments. Pinkish-mauve pointed tepals, darker central bar. Best grown out of strong sunlight to avoid fading. Strong-growing cultivar, free-flowering over long period. Good cut flowers.	Late spring to early autumn	3m (10ft)
'Sunset'	15cm (6in) wide flowers, deep plummy red with purple highlights, yellow anthers. Very good free-flowering cultivar.	Late spring to early autumn	2.5m (8¼ft)
'The President' ♔	Very full flower, 15cm (6in) wide with dark red anthers. Overlapping, rich purple, pointed tepals. Good cut flower & open spiky seed heads. Compact habit, long flowering period, ideal for containers & small gardens.	Late spring to early autumn	3m (10ft)
'The Velvet'	Star-like 18cm (7in) wide flowers with yellow anthers. Overlapping, purple-blue tepals with purple central bar. Tepal reverse has three red veins on a central white band & pale blue edges. Good repeat flowering habit.	Late spring to early summer, and late summer to early autumn	2–3m (6½–10ft)
'Twilight'	Well-rounded 12.5–15cm (5–6in) wide flowers, yellow anthers. Deep mauve-pink tepals with pink shading at base, colour fades gently to light mauve-pink. Compact free-flowering habit, ideal for containers & small gardens.	Late spring to late summer	2.5m (8¼ft)
'Ulrique'	12.5–18cm (5–7in) wide flowers, wine-red anthers. Lavender-violet, pointed, wavy-edged tepals with broad central amethyst bar. Vigorous habit.	Early summer to midsummer, and late summer	2.5m (8¼ft)
Vino™ 'Poulvo'®	Petunia-red flowers, 15–18cm (6–7in) across, yellowy-cream anthers. Later flowers much paler & smaller, 10–12.5cm (4–5in) across. Attractive foliage. Good as a cut flower & for container culture.	Late spring to late summer	3m (10ft)
Vivienne 'Beth Currie'	Well-formed flower, 10–12cm (4–5in) across. Overlapping plum-purple tepals with crimson central bar, reddish-cream anthers. Compact plant, very free-flowering in spring and good crop of later flowers. Ideal for small gardens or containers.	Late spring to early summer, and late summer to early autumn	2.5m (8¼ft)

SPECIES OR CULTIVAR	DESCRIPTION AND OUTSTANDING FEATURES	FLOWERING SEASON IN ENGLAND (see page 78 for months)	HEIGHT
'Wada's Primrose'	15cm (6in) wide flowers with yellow anthers. Creamy-yellow tepals fade to creamy white. Slight primrose scent & medium-sized, spherical seed heads. May be slow growing but thrives in hot climates.	Late spring to early summer	2.5m (8¼ft)
'Warsaw Nike' (syn 'Warszawska Nike')	Rich velvety red-purple flowers, 15cm (6in) across, with pale yellow anthers. Best against a light background. Very free-flowering, generally on new growth but some old-wood flowers.	Early to late summer, and early autumn	2.5–3m (8¼–10ft)
'Will Goodwin'	15cm (6in) wide flowers with bright yellow anthers. Clear mid-blue, overlapping tepals with pointed tips & wavy edges. Flowers very well in late summer. Good cut flower.	Early to late summer, and early autumn	3m (10ft)
'William Kennett'	Fully-rounded flower, 12.5–15cm (5–6in) across, dark red anthers. Pale lavender-blue, pointed, overlapping tepals, wavy-edged when young.	Early to late summer	3m (10ft)

Clematis 'Wada's Primrose', raised in Japan, is very early flowering.

Section 5 – Double and Semi-double Cultivars

The flowers produced by this group often appear rather strange when compared with the single, large-flowered types, especially when the green outer tepals are present. Sometimes, doubles such as 'Belle of Woking' and 'Duchess of Edinburgh' have several layers of green outer tepals before the true coloured tepals are present, forming a rosette-like flower. The fully double flowers are produced from the stems that became ripened the previous season. Some members of this group produce only double flowers, some, double from the old previous season's stems and then single on the current season's growth. Others produce double, semi-double and single all at the same time!

A south or west facing position is best for most cultivars, otherwise many green or unsightly coloured flowers could be produced due to lack of sunlight, especially with the first crop of flowers each spring. If you require green flowers for flower arrangements etc. then a north or east facing position will provide these for you. Due to the heavy nature of the blooms produced by this group of clematis, it is advisable to plant them to grow up through another wall trained shrubs, evergreens are ideal, or free-standing low shrubs or conifers. This will avoid damage by excessive winds or heavy rainstorms when in flower. All plants from this group make ideal container grown clematis for the patio or conservatory. They are mainly early summer flowering (double and semi-double flowers) and mid to late summer (single flowers). Follow the Group Two pruning instructions for all the clematis in this section. Hardiness zone 4-9, unless otherwise stated (see page 78).

SOME OF THE MOST REWARDING CLEMATIS TO GROW IN THIS SUB-GROUP:	Arctic Queen™ 'Evitwo'® 'Daniel Deronda' Josephine™ 'Evijohill'® 'Kiri Te Kanawa'	'Louise Rowe' 'Mrs George Jackman' 'Royalty' 'Walter Pennell'

Clematis Arctic Queen™ 'Evitwo'® is one of the most free-flowering, double clematis.

Midsummer flowers of Clematis 'Jackmanii Rubra'.

Clematis 'Belle of Woking' has silvery, fully double flowers.

SPECIES OR CULTIVAR	DESCRIPTION AND OUTSTANDING FEATURES	FLOWERING SEASON IN ENGLAND (see page 78 for months)	HEIGHT
Arctic Queen™ 'Evitwo'®	Clear creamy-white flowers, 10–18cm (4–7in) across, yellow anthers. Produces double flowers on both old & new growth. Attractive seed heads. The most free-flowering double clematis available. Good foliage, suitable for cut flowers, for containers & for the small garden.	Early summer to early autumn (always double)	3m (10ft)
'Beauty of Worcester'	Early summer flowers, 12.5–15cm (5–6in) wide, deep blue with a hint of red. Late summer single flowers show yellowish-cream anthers. Good colour but a shy grower.	Early summer (double), late summer (single)	2.5m (8¼ft)
'Belle of Woking'	10cm (4in) wide flowers, creamy-white anthers, very fully double in early summer. Small tepals open silvery-mauve & fade gently to silvery-grey. Weak in constitution but good once established. Suitable for containers & cut flowers.	Early to late summer (always double)	2.5m (8¼ft)
'Countess of Lovelace'	Semi-double to double flowers, 12.5cm (5in) wide, yellow anthers. Narrow, pale lavender tepals, very pointed at tips in early summer. Later single flowers slightly gappy & floppy. Ideal for containers.	Early summer (double), late summer (single)	2.5m (8¼ft)
'Daniel Deronda' ♛	Very large, 18–20cm (7–8in) wide early flowers, later flowers smaller. Young tepals deep purple-blue with plummy highlights, fading to purple-blue. Creamy-yellow anthers. Superb seed heads, seed tails form sphere but with added twist, or topknot, at the apex. Strong-growing, flowers well, ideal for containers.	Early summer (semi-double), midsummer to early autumn (single)	2.5m (8¼ft)
'Duchess of Edinburgh'	12.5cm (5 in) wide white flowers, later ones smaller, creamy-white anthers. Early summer flowers can be fully green & all have rows of green outer tepals. Slight scent & good cut flower. Retains foliage later than most large-flowered clematis.	Early summer to early autumn (always double)	2.5–3m (8¼–10ft)

SPECIES OR CULTIVAR	DESCRIPTION AND OUTSTANDING FEATURES	FLOWERING SEASON IN ENGLAND (see page 78 for months)	HEIGHT
'Jackmanii Alba'	Flowers 15cm (6 in) across, pointed tepals, light chocolate-coloured anthers. Outer tepals of early flowers bluish-mauve, often with green highlights & tips. Inner tepals bluish-white. Later flowers (single) creamy bluish-white. Very strong growing.	Early summer (semi-double), midsummer to early autumn (single)	3m (10ft)
'Jackmanii Rubra'	12.5cm (5in) wide flowers, yellow anthers. Semi-double flowers crimson, slightly purple, single flowers clear crimson. Strong-growing & free-flowering once established.	Early summer (semi-double), midsummer to early autumn (single)	2.5m (8¼ft)
Josephine™ 'Evijohill'®	12.5cm (5in) wide flowers. When first opening, early flowers have bronze base tepals tinged with green, & a darker bar. In partial or full sun, colour develops to lilac with a pink bar. Inner tepals slower to open, also tinged with green, narrower central bar. With age outer tepals fall, creating a pompom. No anthers. Grow in shade for green flowers. Excellent for cut flowers, containers & small gardens.	Early summer to early autumn (always double)	2.5m (8¼ft)
'Kathleen Dunford'	Flowers 18cm (7in) across, deep red anthers. Narrow, pointed tepals, purplish-pink becoming mottled & mauve-blue at edges.	Early summer (semi-double), late summer to early autumn (single)	2.5m (8¼ft)
'Kiri Te Kanawa'	Early flowers 15cm (6in) across, later flowers smaller. Deep blue tepals, cream anthers. Fully double on both old & new growth. Very free-flowering, good cut flower & for containers.	Early summer to early autumn (always double)	2.5m (8¼ft)
'Lady Caroline Nevill'	15cm (6in) wide flowers, light chocolate-coloured anthers. Soft mauve-white tepals with mauve bar. Single flowers paler, with overlapping, tapered tepals. Good cut flower.	Early summer (semi-double), mid to late summer (single)	3m (10ft)
'Louise Rowe'	12.5–15cm (5–6in) wide flowers, cream anthers. Colour varies with light level but tepals age from pale mauve to nearly white. Later flowers paler. Occasionally produces double, semi-double & single flowers at the same time. Suitable as a cut flower & for containers.	Early summer (double), mid to late summer (single)	2–2.5m (6½–8¼ft)
'Miss Crawshay'	12.5cm (5in) wide flowers, pale brown anthers. Tepals pink shaded with lilac & a slight bronze-coloured bar. Inner tepals short & narrow. Dark green, very full foliage, retains colour well. Not very free-flowering.	Early summer (semi-double), mid to late summer (single)	2.5m (8¼ft)
'Mrs George Jackman' 🏆	Fully-rounded flowers, 15cm (6in) wide, light brown anthers. Overlapping tepals bright creamy white, tapering to points. Prolific single flowers. Attractive seed heads. Clear fresh foliage. Suitable for containers.	Early summer (semi-double), mid to late summer (single)	2.5m (8¼ft)
'Mrs Spencer Castle'	Soft pink, sometimes tinged with red, flowers 15cm (6in) wide, creamy yellow anthers. Outer tepals long & pointed, inner tepals shorter. Not very free-flowering.	Early summer (semi-double), mid to late summer (single)	3m (10ft)
'Multi Blue'	Well-rounded flowers 15cm (6in) across, no anthers. Deep navy blue outer tepals, blue or reddish-purple blue inner tepals. Inner tepals narrow, producing central tuft. White tips on pointed tepals give spiky appearance. Compact, free-flowering, suitable as a cut flower, for containers or for small gardens.	Early summer (fully double), midsummer to early autumn (fully to semi-double)	2.5m (8¼ft)
'Proteus'	Early flowers 15–20cm (6–8in) across, later flowers smaller, 10–15cm (4–6in). Double flowers may have mixture of green or purple-pink outer tepals. Inner tepals soft pinkish-purple. Semi-double flowers lack green outer tepals. Single flowers soft mauve-pink, pale yellow anthers. Vigorous when fully established. Large leaves. Plant out of full sun but not north-facing.	Early summer (double & semi-double), mid to late summer (single)	3m (10ft)

SPECIES OR CULTIVAR	DESCRIPTION AND OUTSTANDING FEATURES	FLOWERING SEASON IN ENGLAND (see page 78 for months)	HEIGHT
'Royalty' 🏆	Early flowers 10–12.5cm (4–5in) across, rich purple-mauve, with inner tepals more blue. Later, single flowers 7.5cm (3in) across, lighter in colour. Central boss of yellow anthers on purple filaments. Compact, ideal for containers & small gardens. Best in some sun.	Early summer (semi-double), mid to late summer (single)	2m (6½ft)
'Sylvia Denny'	Compact, well-formed, smallish, pure white flowers 10cm (4in) across. Pale yellow anthers. Young foliage often bronze.	Early summer (semi-double), late summer (single)	3m (10ft)
'Veronica's Choice'	Double flowers 15–18cm (6–7in) across, single 10–12.5cm (4–5in) across. Tepals pale mauve-lavender with hints of rose-pink. Outer, overlapping tepals have blunt tips & crimpled edges, looking frilly. Yellow anthers. Primrose scent. Suitable as a cut flower.	Early summer (double), mid to late summer (single)	2.5m (8¼ft)
'Vyvyan Pennell' 🏆	Large, fully double flowers 15–20cm (6–8in) across. Large outer tepals purple-mauve, sometimes tinged with green. Inner tepals rosy-lavender to lilac, fading to deep lilac-mauve. Later single flowers paler, lilac mauve with light brown anthers, attractive seed heads. Large leaves & strong flower stems. Young plants succumb to clematis wilt rather easily. Suitable as a cut flower & for containers but do not plant in north-facing position.	Early summer (double & semi-double), late summer (single)	2.5–3m (8¼–10ft)
'Walter Pennell'	Early flowers 15cm (6in), later 10–12.5cm (4–5in) across, cream anthers. Tepals deep mauve-pink with slightly darker central bar. Good free-flowering plant.	Early summer (semi-double), late summer (single)	2.5m (8¼ft)

Clematis 'Mrs George Jackman', a very free-flowering old cultivar.

Section 6 – Mid-Season Large-Flowered Cultivars

This group produces some of the largest flowers which can measure up to 20cm across. The flowers are not produced in great abundance at one time as with the early large-flowered and double-flowered cultivars, or the later Jackmanii types, but over a long period of time from early summer to Autumn, with most cultivars in this section. Due to their more open habit, they are ideal for growing up into Rhododendrons, Magnolias, and small trees, where they can sprawl about, displaying their flowers amongst their host. Unfortunately, because of this habit not all are ideal for container culture. Follow the Group Two pruning instructions for all the clematis in this section. Hardiness zone 4-9, unless otherwise stated (see page 78).

SOME OF THE MOST REWARDING CLEMATIS TO GROW IN THIS SUB-GROUP:

'General Sikorski'
'Henryi'
'Marie Boisselot'
'Ramona'
'Violet Charm'

Clematis 'Ramona' well established old cultivar raised in the USA.

Clematis 'Belle Nantaise', a strong growing, mid-season, large-flowered cultivar.

Clematis 'General Sikorski' is a holder of the RHS Award of Garden Merit and is free flowering.

SPECIES OR CULTIVAR	DESCRIPTION AND OUTSTANDING FEATURES	FLOWERING SEASON IN ENGLAND (see page 78 for months)	HEIGHT
'Beauty of Richmond'	Well-rounded 18–20cm (7–8in) wide flowers. Pale lavender-blue tepals recurve as flower ages. Large central boss of light chocolate-coloured anthers. Not very free-flowering but dramatic.	Early to late summer	3m (10ft)
'Belle Nantaise'	Rounded but star-like flowers, 18–20cm (7–8in) across. Pointed lavender-blue tepals with crimpled edges. Very prominent yellow anthers, extra long filaments. Later flowers produced in profusion, good cut flower.	Midsummer to early autumn	3m (10ft)
'Blue Ravine'	Early flowers well-formed, 18–20cm (7–8in) across. Later flowers more star-like, tepals more pointed & less overlapping. Lilac-blue tepals suffused with pinkish mauve, red anthers. Very strong-growing, free-flowering plant. Good garden plant, flowers well in hot summers, well known in North America.	Early summer to midsummer, and early autumn	3m (10ft)
'Crimson King'	Crimson-red flower, 15–18cm (6–7in) across, resembles a water-lily when young. Light brown anthers. Shy-flowering plant with occasional semi-double flowers.	Midsummer to late summer	3m (10ft)
'Duchess of Sutherland'	Carmine-red flowers, 12.5cm (5in) across, deep yellow anthers. Tepal texture thin giving speckled appearance. Not very free-flowering. Early flowers may be semi-double.	Midsummer to late summer	3m (10ft)
'Edomurasaki	Early flowers 15–18cm (6–7in) across, later flowers 10–12.5cm (4–5in). Tepals deep purple-blue, anthers red. Poor constitution when young.	Early summer, and late summer to early autumn	3m (10ft)
'Empress of India'	Fully rounded, creamy rose-red flowers, 15–18cm (6–7in) across. Prominent anthers pale creamy yellow. Not very free-flowering but good cut flower.	Midsummer to late summer	3m (10ft)
'Etoile de Malicorne'	Flowers 15–18cm (6–7in) wide, with dark red anthers. Slightly cupped tepals rich purplish-blue with narrow reddish-purple central bar. Tepal colour fades with age. Free-flowering.	Midsummer to early autumn	3m (10ft)
'Fairy Queen'	Very large flowers, 23–25cm (9–10in) across, light brown anthers. Light pink tepals, with rosy pink bar, fading quickly. Strong habit once established.	Early to late summer	3m (10ft)
'General Sikorski' 🏆	Well-rounded flowers, early ones 15cm (6in) across, later smaller but more plentiful. Overlapping tepals mid mauve to deep blue, hint of rose pink at base, yellow anthers. Very good, strong-growing, free-flowering clematis. Good with climbing roses & for cut flowers.	Midsummer to early autumn	3m (10ft)
'Henryi' 🏆	Well-formed white flowers, 15–20cm (6–8in) across, chocolate-brown anthers. Long flowering season, suitable as a cut flower.	Midsummer to mid autumn	3.5m (12ft)
'Lawsoniana'	Star-like flower, 15–20cm (6–8in) across, light chocolate-coloured anthers. Long pointed tepals, lavender-blue with rosy-pink tones. Not free-flowering.	Early to late summer	3m (10ft)

SPECIES OR CULTIVAR	DESCRIPTION AND OUTSTANDING FEATURES	FLOWERING SEASON IN ENGLAND (see page 78 for months)	HEIGHT
'Marie Boisselot' (syn. 'Madame Le Coultre') ♧	Well rounded flower, 15–20cm (6–8in) wide, golden-yellow anthers. Well-formed, overlapping, creamy-white tepals mature to pure white. Foliage good colour, strong in constitution, remains green into autumn. May flower in early winter in mild locations. Good cut flower.	Early summer to late autumn	3.5m (12ft)
'Maureen'	Well-formed flower, 12.5–15cm (5–6in) across, light chocolate-coloured anthers. Intense rich purple tepals, fading slightly with age. Distinctive foliage, rounded leaflets.	Early to late summer	3m (10ft)
'Mrs Bush'	15–20cm (6–8in) wide flowers, prominent light chocolate-coloured anthers. Ridged, narrow, slightly pointed, lavender-blue tepals. Strong healthy foliage but not free-flowering.	Midsummer to early autumn	3.5m (12ft)
'Mrs Hope'	15cm (6in) wide flowers, dark red anthers. Overlapping tepals, pale blue with slightly darker central band. Not free-flowering unless in a sunny location. Profuse foliage often with simple leaves.	Midsummer to early autumn	3.5m (12ft)
'Peveril Pearl'	15–18cm (6–7in) wide flowers, light pinkish-brown anthers. Broad tepals, very pale lavender with rosy highlights, narrower tepals on later flowers. Best against a dark background.	Early summer to early autumn	3m (10ft)
'Prins Hendrik'	Well-rounded flower, somewhat star-shaped, 15–18cm (6–7in) across, dark red anthers. Mid to pale blue tepals with crimpled edges. Good cut flower.	Early to late summer	3m (10ft)
'Ramona'	Well-formed, pale blue flowers, 15–18cm (6–7 in) across, dark red anthers. Strong, healthy foliage, leaves often simple. Flowers best in a sunny location. Most widely grown in USA & Canada.	Early summer to early autumn	3.5m (12ft)
'Serenata'	Gappy flowers, especially later in season, 12.5cm (5in) across, golden-yellow anthers. Dusky dark purple tepals with reddish bar. Free-flowering, good cut flower. Best against light background.	Early summer to early autumn	3m (10ft)
'Torleif'	18cm (7 in) wide flowers with large boss of red anthers on white filaments & prominent white styles. Tepals blue-mauve with marked double central rib, sometimes reddish, twisting with age. Large leaves trifoliate with pointed tips. Large, vigorous plant.	Early to late summer	3m (10ft)
'Violet Charm'	Well-formed flowers, 15–18cm (6–7in) across, red anthers. Pale violet-blue tepals, slightly crimpled edges. Healthy-looking foliage, good cut flower. Very free-flowering, especially later. Good container plant.	Early summer to early autumn	3.5m (12ft)
'W. E. Gladstone'	18–20cm (7–8in) wide pale blue flowers, red anthers. Not free-flowering but long season & good cut flowers. Strong habit once established.	Early summer to early autumn	3.5m (12ft)

Pruning Group Three

Sections 7, 8 & 9

Group Three Pruning Instructions

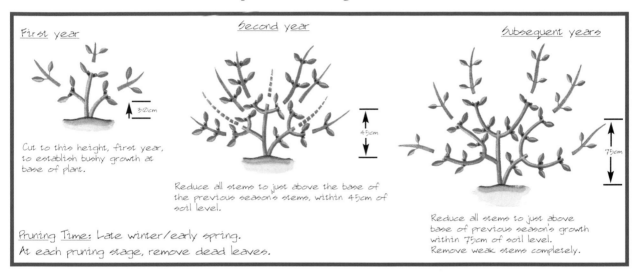

First year

Cut to this height, first year, to establish bushy growth at base of plant.

Pruning Time: Late winter/early spring.
At each pruning stage, remove dead leaves.

Second year

Reduce all stems to just above the base of the previous season's stems, within 45cm of soil level.

Subsequent years

Reduce all stems to just above base of previous season's growth within 75cm of soil level. Remove weak stems completely.

Section 7– Later Flowering Large-Flowered Cultivars

The flowers produced by the clematis in this section are produced on the current season's stems. They are most useful garden plants as they can be grown over and through a great range of objects and hosts. Shrub and species roses as well as climbing roses on posts or walls can be brightened up with the flowers of these clematis. They can also be allowed to clamber about at ground level over low growing shrubs such as helianthemums or even through annual summer bedding plants. These clematis, sadly, do not lend themselves easily to be grown as plants in containers due to the habit of flowering at the end of their growing tips, which would be 2 metres in length. However with careful training of the plant this can be done. Follow the Group Three pruning instructions for all the clematis in this section. Hardiness zone 3-9, unless otherwise stated (see page 78).

SOME OF THE MOST REWARDING CLEMATIS TO GROW IN THIS SUB-GROUP:

'Ascotiensis'
'Comtesse de Bouchaud'
'Dorothy Walton'
'Gipsy Queen'
'Jackmanii'
'John Huxtable'
'Madame Edouard André'
'Perrin's Pride'

'Pink Fantasy'
'Rhapsody'
'Star of India'
'Victoria'

SPECIES OR CULTIVAR	DESCRIPTION AND OUTSTANDING FEATURES	FLOWERING SEASON IN ENGLAND (see page 78 for months)	HEIGHT
'Allanah'	10–12.5cm (4–5in) wide flowers, anthers almost black. Deep bright red blunt-tipped tepals. Produces terminal flowers rather than along stem.	Early summer to early autumn	2.5m (8¼ft)
'Ascotiensis' ♧	12.5cm (5in) wide flowers. greenish-chocolate anthers. Broad tepals bright mid-blue with darker veins. Flowers well along the stem, ideal with roses & good container plant. Very free-flowering & vigorous once established.	Midsummer to early autumn	3m (10ft)
'Blue Angel' (syn. 'Blekitny Aniol')	Pale lavender-blue flowers, 10–12cm (4–4¾in) across, greenish yellow anthers. Flowers produced freely, looks well with roses.	Midsummer to late summer	4m (13ft)
'Cardinal Wyszynski'	Crimson flowers, 10–12.5cm (4–5in) wide, crimson anthers. Best against a light background.	Midsummer to early autumn	2.5m (8¼ft)
'Comtesse de Bouchaud' ♧	Rounded flowers, 12.5cm (5in) wide, cream anthers. Deeply textured, bright mauve-pink tepals with a satin sheen, crimpled edges & blunt tips. Extremely free-flowering & ideal with roses.	Midsummer to early autumn	3m (10ft)
'Dorothy Walton' (syn. 'Bagatelle')	Star-like 12.5cm (5in) wide flowers & coffee-coloured anthers. Very pointed mauve-pink tepals, hint of blue-mauve, colour strongest at edge & centre. Good container plant for late summer colour. Extremely free-flowering plant.	Early summer to early autumn	2.5–3m (8¼–10ft)
'Ernest Markham' ♧	Roundish flowers, 10–12.5cm (4–5in) wide, light brown anthers. Broad, overlapping, magenta tepals, taper to a point, crimpled edges. For most flowers, plant in full sun.	Midsummer to mid autumn	3–4m (10–13ft)
'Gipsy Queen' ♧	Early flowers, 15cm (6in) wide, on very strong stems. Later flowers, 10–12.5cm (4–5in) wide, freely produced . Tepals deep velvety violet-purple, dark red anthers. Flowers on old & new wood.	Early summer to early autumn	3m (10ft)
'Hagley Hybrid'	Rosy-mauve to shell pink flowers, 10cm (4in) wide, pointed tepals & dark red anthers. Flowers fade quickly in full sun. Very free-flowering & compact.	Early summer to late summer	2.5m (8¼ft)
'Honora'	Gappy 18cm (7in) wide flowers, deep purple-red anthers on light purple filaments. Rich purple tepals with deep purple central bar, & crimpled edges. As flower matures, tepals twist & tips recurve. Very free-flowering, excellent with roses.	Early summer to early autumn	3–4m (10–13ft)
'Jackmanii' ♧	Semi-nodding 10cm (4in) wide flowers, borne profusely along stem, creamy green anthers. Deep dark velvet purple tepals, fading to bluish-purple. Leaves generally trifoliate, occasionally simple. Good with roses & any perennial plants.	Midsummer to early autumn	3m (10ft)
'Jackmanii Superba'	Flowers 12.5cm (5in) across, greenish-cream anthers. Tepals broader than 'Jackmanii', almost square, deep rich purple on opening. Leaves generally simple.	Midsummer to early autumn	3m (10ft)
'Jan Pawell II' (syn. 'John Paul II')	Early flowers 12cm (4¾in) wide, later 7.5–10cm (3–4in) wide, dark red anthers. Overlapping tepals tapering to a point, pearly white with a satin sheen. Flowers best in sun though colour will fade to white.	Midsummer to early autumn	3.5m (12ft)
'John Huxtable'	Creamy-white flowers, 10cm (4in) across, yellow-white anthers. Free-flowering, ideal with roses.	Midsummer to late summer.	2.5–3m (8¼–10ft)

SPECIES OR CULTIVAR	DESCRIPTION AND OUTSTANDING FEATURES	FLOWERING SEASON IN ENGLAND (see page 78 for months)	HEIGHT
'Lady Betty Balfour'	15cm (6in) wide flowers, yellow anthers. Broad, overlapping, purple-blue tepals, fading with age. Plant in full sun to obtain flowers. Strong-growing but seems prone to clematis wilt.	Early autumn to mid autumn	3.5m (12ft)
'Lilacina Floribunda'	Early flowers 12.5cm (5in) wide, later flowers smaller, deep red anthers. Pointed, gappy tepals, deep rich purple fading with age. Flowers from both old & new wood, very strong-growing but somewhat untidy plant.	Early summer to early autumn	3m (10ft)
'Madame Baron Veillard'	10–12.5cm (4–5in) flowers, overlapping lilac-rose tepals, greenish anthers. Due to late flowering habit, must be grown in sun to obtain good crop of flowers. Very vigorous, ideal for covering large areas.	Early autumn to mid autumn	3–4m (10–13ft)
'Madame Edouard André' ♉	Slightly cup-shaped 10cm (4in) wide flowers, creamy-yellow anthers. Clear to dusky red, roundish tepals, tapering to a point, fade to mauve-red with age. Compact habit & profuse flowering, ideal for containers, good with herbaceous plants.	Midsummer to late summer	2.5m (8¼ft)
'Madame Grangé' ♉	Flowers 10–12.5cm (4–5in) wide, light brownish-green anthers. Boat-shaped dusky velvet-purple tepals with red-purple central bar & dusky silver reverse. Flowers borne freely along stem to tip, best against a light background.	Midsummer to late summer	3m (10ft)

Clematis 'Pink Fantasy' is compact and extremely free-flowering.

Clematis 'Prince Charles' is ideal for providing summer colour in a container.

SPECIES OR CULTIVAR	DESCRIPTION AND OUTSTANDING FEATURES	FLOWERING SEASON IN ENGLAND (see page 78 for months)	HEIGHT
'Margaret Hunt'	Dusky mauve-pink, 10cm open flowers. Very free flowering, vigorous.	Midsummer to late summer	3m (10ft)
'Perle d'Azure'	Semi-nodding, rounded flowers, 10cm (4in) across, pale yellow anthers. Light blue tepals, hint of pink towards base & on reverse, quite translucent. Free-flowering along stem to tip, subject to mildew in some locations, good with roses.	Early summer to early autumn	3.5m (12ft)
'Perrin's Pride'	Early flowers, 15cm (6in) wide, from old wood, profusion of later flowers on new wood. Well-rounded, bronze-purple tepals recurve slightly, greenish-bronze anthers. Best against a light background.	Early summer to early autumn	3m (10ft)
'Pink Fantasy'	10cm (4in) wide flowers, dusky red anthers. Pink tepals with peachy pink highlights & deeper central bar prominent towards base. Very good, compact, free-flowering plant, ideal for containers & cut flowers.	Midsummer to early autumn	2–2.5m (6¹/₂–8¹/₄ft)
'Prince Charles'	Profuse, semi-nodding 10cm (4in) wide flowers, yellowish-green anthers. Pointed, slightly twisted, mauve-blue tepals, can become greenish-azure blue. Compact, free-flowering plant, ideal for containers & a good cut flower. Sometimes subject to mildew in dry conditions.	Midsummer to early autumn	2–2.5m (6¹/₂–8¹/₄ft)
'Rhapsody'	10–12.5cm (4–5in) flowers, with creamy-yellow anthers splayed open. Sapphire blue tepals deepen in colour with age. Compact, free-flowering plant, ideal for containers.	Early summer to early autumn	2.5–3m (8¹/₄–10ft)
'Romantika' ᴮ C ˢ C of M 1998	Dark violet-purple flowers, 7–10cm (2³/₄–4in) across, yellow anthers. Best in a sunny position, against a light background. Suitable for containers.	Early to late summer	2.5m (8¹/₄ft)
'Rouge Cardinal'	Well-rounded flower, 10cm (4in) wide, brownish-red anthers. Velvety crimson tepals with a surface sheen, fade with age, tips recurve. Very free-flowering though plant constitution is weak & foliage floppy.	Midsummer to late summer	2.5–3m (8¹/₄–10ft)
'Star of India'	10cm (4in) flowers with greenish-cream anthers, borne freely along stem to tip. Tepals squareish, with rounded edges & blunt tips, deep purple-blue with carmine central bar. Associates well with roses.	Midsummer to late summer	3m (10ft)
'Victoria'	10–14cm (4–5¹/₂in) flowers, greenish-yellow anthers. Broad, overlapping, deep rosy-mauve tepals fade to light mauve, soft rosy-purple central bar. Vigorous, free-flowering but needs a light background. Good with roses.	Midsummer to late summer	3m (10ft)
'Ville de Lyon'	Rounded flowers, 10–12.5cm (4–5in) wide, yellow anthers. Rounded, blunt-tipped, overlapping, bright crimson tepals. Wide deepish-pink central bar overlaid by darker veins. Strong-growing, free-flowering clematis. Best grown through evergreen shrubs to hide bare lower stems in midsummer.	Early summer to early autumn	3m (10ft)
'Voluceau'	10cm (4 in) wide flowers with slightly twisted, petunia-red tepals & yellow anthers. Very strong-growing, free-flowering plant, will withstand coastal conditions.	Early summer to late summer	3m (10ft)

Section 8 – Viticella Types

Clematis viticella is a vigorous European species, since its introduction in the 16th century to England, it has given rise to many fine cultivars. *Clematis viticella* 'Purpurea Plena Elegans' is known to have also been in cultivation from about that time, although it is still not commonly grown. This group of clematis, like the large later-flowering types, offer splendid value for money, in addition, they do not suffer at all from clematis wilt. Their colour range is good and their flowering period is from mid summer until autumn. Many have semi-nodding flowers and can be grown in small trees where their flowers can be enjoyed from below, looking up into the flowers. They look equally good tumbling about through shrubs of any height, even scrambling around at ground level on low-growing ground cover plants such as winter and summer flowering heathers. Follow the Group Three pruning instructions for all the clematis in this section. Hardiness zone 3-9, unless otherwise stated (see page 78).

Clematis viticella 'Abundance'

SOME OF THE MOST REWARDING CLEMATIS TO GROW IN THIS SUB-GROUP:

viticella 'Abundance'
viticella 'Alba Luxurians'
viticella 'Betty Corning'
viticella 'Etoile Violette'
viticella 'Madame Julia Correvon'

viticella 'Polish Spirit'
viticella 'Purpurea Plena Elegans'
viticella 'Royal Velours'
viticella 'Venosa Violacea'

SPECIES OR CULTIVAR	DESCRIPTION AND OUTSTANDING FEATURES	FLOWERING SEASON IN ENGLAND (see page 78 for months)	HEIGHT
campaniflora	Nodding, open bell-shaped flowers, 2–2.5cm (³/₄–1in) across, creamy green anthers. Tepals white to pale blue, recurving at tips & twisting slightly with age. Slightly glaucous foliage and leaves divided into many leaflets. Hardiness zone 4-9.	Midsummer to late summer	4.5m (15ft)
campaniflora 'Lisboa'	Larger flowers, 5cm (2in) across, greenish-yellow anthers. Purple-blue tepals recurve at tips. Vigorous, showy plant, good with large blue-foliage conifers. Hardiness zone 4-9.	Midsummer to early autumn	4.5m (15ft)
viticella	Nodding or semi-nodding open bell-shaped, mauve flowers, 3cm (1¹/₄in) across. Flowers profusely borne on new growth, normally about 3m (10ft). Neither the species nor any of its cultivars succumb to clematis wilt.	Midsummer to early autumn	3m (10ft)
viticella 'Abundance'	Semi-nodding, flat open flowers, 5–7.5cm (2–3in) across, yellowish anthers. Heavily textured wine rose tepals, recurve at tips & along edges. Very free-flowering.	Midsummer to early autumn	3m (10ft)
viticella 'Alba Luxurians'	Nodding, flat open flowers, 7.5cm (3in) across, purple-black anthers. White tepals, green at tip in midsummer, earliest flowers have more green. Slightly glaucous foliage. Vigorous plant. Good cut flowers.	Midsummer to early autumn	3m (10ft)

SPECIES OR CULTIVAR	DESCRIPTION AND OUTSTANDING FEATURES	FLOWERING SEASON IN ENGLAND (see page 78 for months)	HEIGHT
viticella 'Betty Corning'	Nodding bell-shaped flowers, 5–6cm (2–2¼n) long, pale yellow anthers. Tepals light pinkish-mauve inside, pale pinkish-blue on reverse, paler central bar. Scented.	Midsummer to mid autumn	2m (6½ft)
viticella 'Blue Belle'	Well-rounded, semi-nodding flowers, 9cm (3½in) across, yellow anthers. Deep violet-purple tepals. Useful for its large flowers, good as a cut flower. Strong-growing, free-flowering plant.	Midsummer to early autumn	3.5m (12ft)
viticella 'Carmencita'	Nodding flowers, 6cm (2¼in) across, black anthers. Tepals carmine with a satin texture. Free-flowering, ideal grown into small tree to view flowers from below.	Midsummer to early autumn	3.5m (12ft)
viticella 'Etoile Violette' 🏆	Nodding or semi-nodding, slightly gappy flowers, 7–8cm (2¾–3¼in) wide. Tepals violet-purple with a reddish tint when young, recurving at edges. Anthers yellow. Vigorous, very free-flowering plant, best against a light background.	Midsummer to early autumn	3–4m (10–13ft)
viticella 'Kermesina'	Semi-nodding flowers 6cm (2¼in) across, anthers almost black. Tepals recurve at edges, a deep rich red with a white blotch at base. Free-flowering plant, good with a grey background.	Midsummer to early autumn	3m (10ft)
viticella 'Little Nell'	Semi-nodding creamy bluish-white flowers, up to 5cm (2in) across, greenish-yellow anthers. Suitable for scrambling at ground level.	Midsummer to early autumn	3m (10ft)
viticella 'Madame Julia Correvon' 🏆	Profuse, semi-nodding, gappy flowers, 7cm (2¾in) wide, splayed open pale yellow anthers. Vibrant, rich red tepals, recurving at tip, twisting with age. Tepal reverse pale pink with white central bar. Reasonably compact habit, free-flowering, can be container grown. Good with roses or grey foliage plants & as a cut flower.	Midsummer to early autumn	3m (10ft)
viticella 'Margot Koster'	Semi-nodding, gappy flowers, 10cm (4in) wide, greenish-yellow anthers. Deep mauve-pink tepals recurve at edges & roll back on themselves. Very free-flowering plant. Good with grey foliage plants, blue flowers & roses.	Midsummer to early autumn	3.5m (12ft)
viticella 'Minuet' 🏆	Semi-nodding flowers, 6cm (2¼in) wide, blackish anthers. Blunt-tipped tepals with base colour of white veined pale purplish-red on edges. Grow into small trees to view flowers from below, or on ground with heathers. Good cut flower.	Midsummer to early autumn	3m (10ft)
viticella 'Polish Spirit' 🏆	Semi-nodding flowers, 7cm (2¾in) wide, blackish-red anthers. Very intense purple-blue tepals have satin sheen when young. Too vigorous & dense to grow with ground-cover but good with large shrubs or small trees. Outstanding plant, very free-flowering, very good foliage retained in summer. Good as cut flowers.	Midsummer to early autumn	3–4m (10–13ft)
viticella 'Purpurea Plena' (syn. 'Mary Rose')	Fully double, sterile, smoky bluish-mauve, nodding flowers, 5cm (2in) across. Free-flowering once established, needs a light background.	Midsummer to early autumn	3m (10ft)

SPECIES OR CULTIVAR		DESCRIPTION AND OUTSTANDING FEATURES	FLOWERING SEASON IN ENGLAND *(see page 78 for months)*	HEIGHT
viticella 'Purpurea Plena Elegans'	♆	Fully double, sterile, dusky violet-purple nodding flowers, 6–7cm (2¹/₄–2³/₄in) across. Outer tepals occasionally green or green at tips. Looks good with very pale green or grey foliage shrubs & small trees. Useful cut flower, picked in long strands for pedestals.	Midsummer to early autumn	3.5m (12ft)
viticella 'Royal Velours'	♆	Semi-nodding flowers, 5cm (2in) across, greenish-black anthers. Deep velvety-purple, rounded tepals with a satin sheen & recurved tips. Must have a light background, good with light grey foliage. Good cut flower.	Midsummer to early autumn	3m (10ft)
viticella 'Södertälje' (syn. *v.* 'Grandiflora Sanguinea')		Semi-nodding, slightly gappy flowers, 8cm (3¹/₄in) wide, light green anthers. Pinkish-red tepals recurve at tips. Strong-growing plant, well-suited to pine trees.	Midsummer to early autumn	3m (10ft)
viticella 'Tango'		Semi-nodding flowers, 7.5cm (3in) wide, dark red anthers. Greenish-cream tepals with deep mauve pink veins towards edges. Similar to 'Minuet' but larger flowers & brighter colouring.	Midsummer to early autumn	3m (10ft)
viticella 'Venosa Violacea'	♆	Very full, semi-nodding flowers, 10cm (4in) across, black anthers. Overlapping, boat-shaped tepals, white with purple veins becoming darker towards edge. Veins intensify & cover whole tepal in hot weather. Free-flowering, very long flowering season in mild climates. Good cut flower.	Midsummer to mid autumn	2–3m (6¹/₂–10ft)

Clematis viticella 'Södertälje' (left) and Clematis viticella 'Blue Belle' (right) are both typical examples of the viticella types that love to tumble through shrubs or scramble at ground level.

Section 9 – Late-Flowered Species and Cultivars

This group, which is quite variable, consists of the clematis species and their forms or cultivars which produce flowers on the current season's stems. They are basically mid to late summer or autumn flowering and can be used to enhance a large range of host plants, objects, large trees and large or small wall areas. With a few exceptions, these are all too vigorous for container culture. Details given with each plant will assist in the selection for the most suitable host. Follow the Group Three pruning instructions for all the clematis in this section. Hardiness zone 4-9 unless otherwise stated (see page 78).

SOME OF THE MOST REWARDING CLEMATIS TO GROW IN THIS SUB-GROUP:

× *aromatica*
'Blue Boy'
'Durandii'
florida 'Sieboldii'
florida 'Plena'
'Huldine'
integrifolia var. *integrifolia*
integrifolia 'Pangborne Pink'
Petit Faucon™ 'Evisix'®
recta var. *recta*
rehderiana

tangutica 'Bill Mackenzie'
terniflora
texensis 'Duchess of Albany'
texensis 'Sir Trevor Lawrence'
tibetana var. *vernayi* 'L & S' 13342
× *triternata* 'Rubromarginata'
viorna

Clematis integrifolia 'Alba' is a herbaceous plant with good scent.

This unusual species is Clematis viorna which has attractive seed heads.

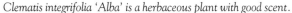

SPECIES OR CULTIVAR	DESCRIPTION AND OUTSTANDING FEATURES	FLOWERING SEASON IN ENGLAND (see page 78 for months)	HEIGHT
addisonii	Nodding, pitcher-shaped flowers, 3cm (1¼in) long. Tepals purple to red with creamy edges, recurved tips. Glaucous foliage, sometimes subject to mildew. Low growing, non-clinging plant, suitable for the mixed border. Hardiness zone 7-9.	Midsummer to early autumn	60cm (2ft)
aethusifolia	Creamy-yellow bell-shaped flowers, 2cm (¾in) long, tips recurve, greenish-yellow anthers. Daphne scent. Free-flowering especially in sunny location. Attractive foliage, pale green leaflets deeply dissected, fern-like. Non-clinging. Hardiness zone 6-9.	Late summer to early autumn	2m (6½ft)

SPECIES OR CULTIVAR	DESCRIPTION AND OUTSTANDING FEATURES	FLOWERING SEASON IN ENGLAND (see page 78 for months)	HEIGHT
akebioides	Open bell-shaped flowers, 4cm (1½in) across, greenish-brown anthers. Yellow tepals generally tinged on top with greenish-bronze or purple. Thick, fleshy, glaucous, pinnate leaves.	Midsummer to mid autumn	4m (13ft)
'Alionushka' ᴮCₒₛⱼ C of M 1998	Semi-nodding to nodding flowers, 6–8cm (2¼–3¼in) long, cream anthers Rich, slightly mauve-pink tepals, satin sheen when young. Deep ridges on tepal reverse, crumpled edges, tips recurve & twist with age. Strong, healthy, coarse-textured foliage. Semi-herbaceous, non-clinging, good for a mixed border.	Midsummer to early autumn	1–1.5m (3¼–5ft)
'Arabella'	Round, semi-nodding flowers, 7–8cm (2¾–3¼in) wide. Rosy purple tepals flushed with red. Creamy anthers. Non-clinging, very free-flowering.	Midsummer to early autumn	2m (6½ft)
× *aromatica*	Gappy, star-like dark velvet purple flowers, 3–4cm (1¼–1½in) wide. Creamy-yellow anthers. Strong vanilla scent. Non-clinging, very dark green pinnate leaves. Needs light background, good with grey shrubs.	Early summer to early autumn	2m (6½ft)
'Blue Boy'	Semi-nodding to nodding 5–7cm (2–2¾in) wide pale blue flowers, tepal tips recurve. Non-clinging, very free-flowering, good mixed border plant. Hardiness zone 3-9.	Midsummer to early autumn	2m (6½ft)
brachiata	Semi-nodding to nodding, 2–3cm (¾–1¼in) deep flowers, slightly scented. Recurving white to creamy-green tepals reveal a large boss of yellow anthers. Hardiness zone 8-9.	Late summer to mid autumn	5m (16½ft)
brevicaudata	Scented, star-shaped creamy-white flowers, 2cm (¾in) across, creamy-yellow anthers. Hardiness zone 5-9.	Late summer to mid autumn	4–5m (13–16½ft)
connata	Bell-like, creamy-yellow flowers, 3–4cm (1¼–1½in) long, creamy-green anthers. Some forms open widely, other closer with just tips recurving. Very vigorous, leaves have paired petiole bases forming large disc-shape at nodes. Very late flowering, needs full sun for good crop of flowers. Hardiness zone 6-9.	Early to mid autumn	5m (16½ft)
crispa	Nodding pitcher-shaped flowers, 3–4cm (1¼–1½in) long. Tepals lavender to purple, recurving at tips, tepal edges crispulate & almost white. Native habitat marshland, sometimes acid soil, but grows well in normal garden soil. Hardiness zone 5-9.	Midsummer to late summer	2m (6½ft)
'Durandii'	Semi-nodding, gappy, flat open flowers, 8–10cm (3½–4in) across, good cut flower. Indigo-blue tepals deeply ribbed, pointed at tip, deep mid-blue on reverse. Cream anthers, filaments white, blue at base. Simple lanceolate leaves. Non-clinging habit, good with ground cover plants.	Midsummer to early autumn	1–2m (3¼–6½ft)
'Eriostemon'	Semi-nodding, semi-open flowers, 5–6cm (2–2¼in) across, greenish-cream anthers. Tepals purple-blue, satin sheen when young, recurve at tips. Non-clinging, strong-growing, very free-flowering, good for mixed border & containers. Hardiness zone 3-9.	Midsummer to early autumn	2m (6½ft)
flammula	Star-like white flowers, 2.5cm (1in) across, produced extremely profusely. Tepals narrow & blunt tipped. Anthers creamy-white. Strong almond scent. Best in well-drained soil, sunny location. Attractive seed heads. Hardiness zone 6-9.	Midsummer to early autumn	4.5m (15ft)

SPECIES OR CULTIVAR	DESCRIPTION AND OUTSTANDING FEATURES	FLOWERING SEASON IN ENGLAND (see page 78 for months)	HEIGHT
florida **Pistachio**™ 'Evirida'®	Rounded flower, 8cm (3¼in) across. Overlapping tepals creamy-white in summer, creamy green in autumn. In flower centre, pinkish-grey anthers & green tuft of aborted stigmas. Extremely free-flowering over a long period. Best grown through wall-trained shrubs, but good in containers & for cut flowers. Hardiness zone 6-9.	Early summer to early autumn outside, until late autumn under glass	3m (10ft)
florida 'Plena'	Rosette-like, full double flowers, 10cm (4in) across. Overlapping outer tepals creamy-white in summer to greenish-white in late autumn. in the centre, numerous small, pointed tepals. Best in sheltered site. Grow through evergreen shrubs or in containers. Good cut flower, singly or in strands. Hardiness zone 6-9.	Early summer to early autumn outside, until late autumn under glass	2–3m (6½–10ft)
florida 'Sieboldii'	Fully-rounded flowers, 10cm (4in) across. Overlapping outer tepals, creamy-white in summer, creamy-green in autumn, tips recurve. Central boss of purple petaloid stamens 5–6cm (2–2¼in) across. Best in sheltered site, grow through wall-trained shrubs or in containers. Good cut flower. Hardiness zone 6-9.	Early summer to early autumn outside, until late autumn under glass	2–3m (6½–10ft)
fruticosa	Semi-noddng, semi-open flowers, 5cm (2in) across, borne in small clusters. Yellow tepals recurve at tips. Red anthers. Dark green lanceolate leaves. Closely branched plant, useful in mixed border. Hardiness zone 5-9.	Midsummer to early autumn	60cm (2ft)
fusca var. *fusca*	Bell-shaped flowers, 2–3cm (¾–1¼in) long, hang downwards from leaf axils. Thick-textured brown tepals, covered in thick downy brown hairs. Inner surface of tepals, cream or occasionally light blue, shown as tips recurve. Creamy-green anthers. Leaves pinnatisect, leaflets stalked. Some short forms self-supporting. Interesting in a mixed border or through other plants. Hardiness zone 5-9.	Mid to late summer	1–2m (3¼–6½ft)
fusca var. *violacea*	Larger flowers, 3–5cm (1¼–2in) long, not as hairy as species. Flowers semi-nodding to nodding, open bell-shaped, creamy green anthers. Thick-textured tepals purple-brown, tips recurve to show purple-blue inside. Very large seed heads turn orange as they ripen. Needs a light background. Good in a mixed border, or through other plants. Hardiness zone 5-9.	Midsummer to early autumn	2–3m (6½–10ft)
Golden Tiara® 'Kugotia'	Open bell-shaped flowers, 7cm (2¾in) across, held upright to show full face. Bright yellow recurving tepals, purple anthers, attractive seed heads. Winter hardy. Good with low-growing shrubs, groundcover plants & in containers. Hardiness zone 3-9.	Midsummer to mid autumn	2–3m (6½–10ft)
heracleifolia var. *heracleifolia*	Hyacinth-like, 2cm (¾in) long flowers, some have hyacinth scent. Flower colour can be pink or blue, light or dark. Some forms tepals open fully, some remain closed, giving bell-like tubular flower. Tepals recurve at tips showing creamy-green anthers. Leaves large & coarse, divided into three, serrated-edged leaflets. Herbaceous sub-shrub with woody basal stems, forms huge clump of growth. Good in a mixed border. Hardiness zone 5-9.	Midsummer to mid autumn	1m (3¼ft)
heracleifolia 'Cote d'Azure'	Pale blue, tubular flowers, 2cm (¾in) long. Flowers borne in clusters on long flower stalks up to 15cm (6in). Good cut flower. Base slightly more woody than species, leaflets not so serrated. Attractive seed heads. Hardiness zone 5-9.	Late summer to mid autumn	75cm (2½ft)
heracleifolia var. *davidiana*	Pale powdery blue flowers, 2cm (¾in) long, sweetly scented. Flowers borne tightly in leaf axil buds & terminal buds. Good for cutting. Does not have woody base. Leaves scented when dry in late autumn. Hardiness zone 5-9.	Late summer to mid autumn	90cm (3ft)

SPECIES OR CULTIVAR	DESCRIPTION AND OUTSTANDING FEATURES	FLOWERING SEASON IN ENGLAND (see page 78 for months)	HEIGHT
heracleifolia var. *davidiana* 'Wyevale'	Flowers darker blue & larger than C. heracleifolia var davidiana, 3cm (1¼in) long. Strong hyacinth scent. Good cut flowers. Hardiness zone 5-9.	Midsummer to mid autumn	1–1.2m (3¼–4ft)
hirsutissima var. *scottii* (syn. *douglasii* var. *scottii*)	Nodding bell-shaped flowers, 4cm (1½in) long. Thick, pubescent, mauve blue tepals, reflexed at tip. Lower leaves simple, upper pinnate, young shoots pubescent becoming glaucous. Non-climbing, herbaceous plant. Best in sunny, well-drained site, especially mixed border. Hardiness zone 6-9.	Midsummer to early autumn	45cm (18in)
'Huldine'	Cup-shaped, rounded flowers with yellow anthers, 8cm (3¼in) across, held upright. Inner surface of tepals pearly white, reverse three deep red-purple bars, paler at edges. Tepals almost translucent, mid-ribs show when light shines through. Very strong-growing, long flowering. Good cut flower. Best in sunny position.	Late summer to late autumn in mild localities	5–6m (16½–20ft)
integrifolia var. *integrifolia*	Bell-shaped flowers, 4cm (1½in) deep. Mauve blue to deep blue, pointed, recurving tepals. Attractive seed heads. Simple elliptic leaves which clasp the stem. Non-clinging, herbaceous plant.	Midsummer to late summer	60cm (2ft)
integrifolia 'Alba'	Pure white scented flowers, 4cm (1½in) deep. Variable, so purchase plant in flower to ensure good scented white clone.	Midsummer to late summer	60cm (2ft)
integrifolia 'Pangbourne Pink'	Open bell-shaped, deep pink flowers, 5–6cm (2–2¼in) deep. Large leaves. Large-flowered selection of *integrifolia* 'Rosea'.	Midsummer to late summer	60cm (2ft)
integrifolia 'Rosea'	Variable, flowers 4cm (1½in) deep, pale pink or mauve-pink.	Midsummer to late summer	60cm (2ft)
× *jouiniana* 'Praecox' ♆	Open flowers, 3cm (1¼in), creamy-white anthers. Reflexed tepals, a mixture of bluish-white and mauve. Free-flowering, borne in clusters from leaf axil buds & terminal stems. Useful to cover concrete slabs or old tree stumps, or tied onto walls. Hardiness zone 3-9.	Midsummer to mid autumn	Grown on a wall 3m (10ft), grown at ground level 50cm (20in)
ligusticifolia	Star-like white flowers, 3cm (1¼in) across, unisexual, borne in panicles. Open boss of stamens with white styles. Rather coarse, tough foliage. Vigorous, rather invasive once established. Useful woodland plant. Hardiness zone 5-9.	Late summer to mid autumn	7m (23ft)
'Mrs Robert Brydon'	Bluish-white, open, gappy flowers, 3cm (1¼in) across, cream anthers. Flowers in clusters from leaf axil buds, very free-flowering. Coarse foliage. Strong, vigorous growth from woody stems, sub-shrub habit. Allow to scramble at ground level or tie up into a tree. Hardiness zone 5-9.	Midsummer to mid autumn	3m (10ft)
orientalis	Bell-shaped, nodding flowers, 3cm (1¼in), brown anthers with red filaments. Yellow or yellowish-green tepals. Free-flowering. Glaucous foliage. Hardiness zone 6-9.	Midsummer to early autumn	2–3m (6½–10ft)
'Paul Farges' Summer Snow (syn. × *fargesioides* 'Summer Snow')	Creamy-white, star-like flower, 4cm (1½in) wide, creamy-white anthers. Slightly scented, very free-flowering. Vigorous, ideal to cover walls, buildings, or into trees. Hardiness zone 3-9.	Midsummer to mid autumn	7m (23ft)
Petit Faucon™ 'Evisix'® B C S C of M 1998	Intense deep blue, nodding flowers, 7–9cm (2¾–3½in) long. Tepals twist as flower opens, revealing orange/yellow boss of stamens. Simple elliptic leaves, bronze-green when young, green when mature. Non-clinging. Free-flowering over a long period. Good cut flower, seed heads & good mixed border plant.	Midsummer to early autumn	1m (3¼ft)

SPECIES OR CULTIVAR	DESCRIPTION AND OUTSTANDING FEATURES	FLOWERING SEASON IN ENGLAND (see page 78 for months)	HEIGHT
pitcheri	Pitcher-shaped flowers, 3–4cm (1¼–1½in) long. Thick, violet-purple tepals, recurve at tips to show green-yellow inside. Strong-growing, free-flowering. Best against a light background.	Midsummer to early autumn	3m (10ft)
potaninii var. *fargesii*	Rounded white flowers, 4cm (1½in) wide, yellow anthers. Broad, blunt-tipped, gappy tepals. Good with dark, evergreen foliage plants. Hardiness zone 3-9.	Midsummer to early autumn	3–5m (10–16½ft)
recta var. *recta*	White, narrow tepals making star-like flower, 2 -3cm (1-1¼in) across, creamy-white anthers. Attractive seed heads. Some clones very heavily hawthorn scented. Herbaceous habit. Hardiness zone 3-9.	Midsummer to early autumn	1–2m (3¼–6½ft)
recta var. *purpurea*	Purple-leaved form of species, also with attractive seed heads. Leaves slowly turn green by end of summer unless regularly trimmed & not allowed to flower. Hardiness zone 3-9.	Midsummer to early autumn	1m (3¼ft)
rehderiana ♆	Slightly scented, cowslip-like pendulous flowers, 2-3cm (1-1¼in) deep, produced in panicles. Tepals pale yellow to pale greenish-yellow, especially when young. Very vigorous, stems angular, leaves densely covered with hairs. Attractive seed heads. Hardiness zone 6-9.	Midsummer to mid autumn	5–7m (16½–23ft)
serratifolia	Nodding yellow flowers, 3–4cm (1¼–1½in) wide, fluffy seed heads. Tepals lanceolate to elliptic, spreading open to reveal dark anthers. Bright green leaves. Free-flowering, dense habit, good groundcover. Hardiness zone 3-9.	Midsummer to mid autumn	3–4m (10–13ft)
stans	Unisexual, tubular flowers. 2–3cm (¾–1¼in) long, in clusters in terminal panicles. Tepal colour varies from pale lavender blue to very pale blue, tepals reflex at tips. Sub-shrub with stout stems & trifoliate, veined leaves. Useful mixed border plant.	Midsummer to early autumn	1m (3¼ft)
tangutica var. *tangutica*	Golden-yellow lantern-shaped flowers, 3–4cm (1¼–1½in) long, do not open fully. Large fluffy seed heads. Bright green leaves with serrated margins. Useful garden plant for large walls or open trees. Good cut flower.	Midsummer to late autumn	5–6m (16½–20ft)
tangutica 'Aureolin' ♆	Larger flowers than the species, 5cm (2in) yellow, cowbell-like flowers.	Midsummer to mid autumn	4–5m (13–16½ft)
tangutica 'Bill Mackenzie' ♆	Flower opens more than the species, maturing to an open bell-shaped flower. Flowers 6–7cm (2¼–2¾in) across. Yellow tepals broad with pointed tips. Brownish-yellow-green anthers on reddish filaments. Strong-growing, good cut flower. Best in group for flowers & seed heads.	Midsummer to late autumn	5–6m (16½–20ft)
tangutica 'Burford Variety'	Yellow flowers more rounded than species, 4cm (1½in) long. Good free-flowering cultivar.	Midsummer to mid autumn	3–4m (10–13ft)
tangutica 'Helios'	4–6cm (1½–2¼in) long flowers, lantern-like when young, flat open when mature. Yellow tepals, creamy-yellow anthers, reddish-brown-purple filaments, large seed heads. Compact cultivar, useful for small gardens.	Midsummer to mid autumn	1.5m (5ft)
tangutica var. *obtusiuscula*	Rich yellow, globular flowers open more widely than the species, 3cm (1¼in) long. More compact in habit, smaller leaves, useful for small gardens. Hardiness zone 5-9.	Midsummer to mid autumn	3–4m (10–13ft)
terniflora	Hawthorn-scented star-like flowers, 2-3cm (1-1¼in) wide, narrow white tepals, white anthers. Produced profusely in panicles, followed by silky seed heads. Good cut flower. Well used in North America but needs a long, hot summer to flower well in Britain. Vigorous plant, deciduous in cold climates, evergreen in mild locations. Hardiness zone 5-9.	Late summer to mid autumn	6m (20ft)

SPECIES OR CULTIVAR	DESCRIPTION AND OUTSTANDING FEATURES	FLOWERING SEASON IN ENGLAND (see page 78 for months)	HEIGHT
terniflora 'Robusta'	Larger flowers than species, 5cm (2in) across, broader white tepals, still star-like. Creamy-white anthers. Strong hawthorn scent. Extremely vigorous form of species. Large leaves may have silver stripes down leaflets. Needs sunny, well-drained site to flower well. Hardiness zone 5-9.	Late summer to mid autumn	7m (23ft)
texensis	Flowers semi-nodding, pitcher-shaped 3–4cm (1¼–1½in) long, narrowing towards mouth. Flower colour variable, scarlet-red clones being most sought after. Very thick tepals with recurving pointed tips, may be creamy-yellow inside. Leaves glaucous, pinnate & tough textured, terminal leaflet may become a tendril. Herbaceous plant growing from soil-level each year, almost perennial in habit. Very hardy, sometimes subject to powdery mildew & difficult to establish.	Midsummer to mid autumn	2m (6½ft)
texensis 'Duchess of Albany' 🏆	Upright miniature tulip-like flowers, 5–6cm (2–2¼in) long, pinkish anthers. Tepals pink outside, satiny deep candy-pink inside with darker central bar. Free-flowering. Thick flower stalk gives long-lasting quality as cut flower. Best grown at ground level to look into flowers. Hardiness zone 3-9.	Midsummer to early autumn	3m (10ft)
texensis 'Etoile Rose'	Nodding to semi-nodding deeply textured 6cm (2¼in) flowers. Inside base colour vibrant, pale scarlet-pink, paler towards edges. Outside deep satiny pink. Tepal edges serrated, tips reflex more as mature to show pale yellow anthers. Good cut flower. Very free-flowering, sometimes subject to powdery mildew.	Midsummer to early autumn	2.5–3m (8¼–10ft)

Clematis tibetana ssp vernayi 'L & S' 13342

SPECIES OR CULTIVAR	DESCRIPTION AND OUTSTANDING FEATURES	FLOWERING SEASON IN ENGLAND (see page 78 for months)	HEIGHT
texensis 'Gravetye Beauty'	Miniature tulip-like flowers open to become gappy later, 6–8cm (2¼–3¼in) across. Very deep rich red tapering tepals, recurve as mature to show reddish-brown anthers. Best grown at ground level through groundcover plants or summer bedding plants. Good cut flower.	Midsummer to early autumn	3m (10ft)
texensis 'Ladybird Johnson'	Miniature tulip-like flowers, 4cm (1½in) long, creamy anthers. Deep-textured tepals deep purple-red with a brighter crimson central bar.	Midsummer to early autumn	3m (10ft)
texensis 'Pagoda'	Open, nodding 4–6cm (1½–2¼in) wide flowers, green-cream anthers. Tepals creamy pink-mauve outside, with deeper mauve-purple band. Creamy pink inside, deeper at edges, veined throughout. Flowers equally attractive viewed from above or below.	Midsummer to early autumn	2–3m (6½–10ft)
texensis 'Princess Diana' (syn. *texensis* 'The Princess of Wales')	Miniature tulip-like flowers, 6cm (2¼in) long. Tepals whitish-pink outside, with deep pink central bar. Tepals luminous pink inside, with deep vibrant pink central bar mauve-deep pink at edge.	Mid to late summer, and early autumn	2.5m (8¼ft)
texensis 'Sir Trevor Lawrence'	Miniature tulip-like flowers, 5–6cm (2–2¼in) long, yellow boss of anthers. Outside of tepals whitish-pink in shade, reddish-pink in full sun, with reddish-pink veins. Inside of tepals dusky purple-red, with scarlet central band. Good cut flower. Best grown at ground or eye level. Good with white summer-flowering heathers.	Midsummer to early autumn	3m (10ft)
tibetana var. *tibetana*	Nodding, open, bell-shaped, yellow to greenish-yellow flowers, 4cm (1½in) across. Tips of pointed tepals reflex, opening more as flower matures. Glaucous, leathery leaves. Hardiness zone 5-9.	Midsummer to mid autumn	3–4m (10–13ft)
tibetana var. *vernayi*	Nodding 4–5cm (1½–2in) wide flowers, dark purple anthers. Thick, fleshy tepals, yellow or greenish-yellow splashed with rusty bronze or purple-brown on outside. Hardiness zone 5-9.	Midsummer to early autumn	2–3m (6½–10ft)
tibetana var. *vernayi* 'L & S' 13342 ♔	Nodding flowers globular when young, maturing to open bell-shape, 4cm (1½in) across. Pointed tepals yellow & as thick as lemon rind. Foliage very glaucous & finely-cut. Useful garden plant, especially with rhododendrons. Hardiness zone 5-9.	Midsummer to mid autumn	3m (10ft)
× *triternata* 'Rubromarginata' ♔	Star-like flowers, white with wine edges, 3–4cm (1¼ -1½in) across, creamy anthers. Vigorous when fully established. Very free-flowering. Strong hawthorn scent. Hardiness zone 5-9.	Midsummer to early autumn	3–4m (10–13ft)
viorna	Pendulous, pitcher-shaped flowers, 3–4cm (1¼–1½in) deep, yellow anthers. Thick tepals recurve revealing creamy-yellow edges. Tepal colour varies from violet to dull purple to pink.	Midsummer to early autumn	2m (6½ft)
virginiana	Star-shaped gappy white flowers, 3cm (1¼in) wide, boss of white stamens. Vigorous, rampant plant, ideal for woodland or natural garden but not average garden.	Late summer to mid autumn	7–8m (23–26ft)
vitalba	Creamy-white, star-like, gappy flowers, 2–3cm (1–1¼in) across, creamy-yellow anthers. Excellent seed heads, silky when young, fluffy & greyish-brown when mature. Seed heads look wonderful on frosty mornings & dry well for winter decorations. Very vigorous & free-flowering, almost unruly, naturalizes easily. The only species native to the British Isles, commonly known as 'Old Man's Beard'.	Late summer to early autumn	10m (33ft)

Index

Notes: C.—Clematis; **bold page numbers** refer to illustrations.

Clematis 'Dr Ruppel' and Clematis 'Gypsy Queen' growing in a container and flowering in the late summer. These clematis belong to different pruning groups but in this instance have been treated as Pruning Group 3 to achieve late summer colour.